THE SPORTING ROUGHSHOOT

THE
SPORTING
ROUGHSHOOT

Michael Brander

PELHAM BOOKS
Stephen Greene Press

PELHAM BOOKS/STEPHEN GREENE PRESS
Published by the Penguin Group
27 Wrights Lane, London W8 5TZ, England
Viking Penguin Inc., 40 West 23rd Street, New York, New York 10010, USA
The Stephen Greene Press, 15 Muzzey Street, Lexington, Massachusetts, USA
Penguin Books Australia Ltd, Ringwood, Victoria, Australia
Penguin Books Canada Ltd, 2801 John Street, Markham, Ontario, Canada L3R 1B4
Penguin Books (NZ) Ltd, 182–190 Wairau Road, Auckland 10, New Zealand

Penguin Books Ltd, Registered Offices: Harmondsworth, Middlesex, England

First published 1989

Typeset in 11/13 pt Plantin Light,
printed and bound in Great Britain by
Butler & Tanner Ltd, Frome and London

A CIP catalogue record for this book
is available from the British Library.

ISBN 0 7207 1810 4

For Mackie and Donna

Contents

Preface and Acknowledgements   ix

 1 The Sporting Roughshoot   1
 2 Requisites and Prerequisites   18
 3 Grouse and the Moorland Roughshoot   33
 4 Partridges on the Roughshoot   49
 5 Pheasants on the Roughshoot   64
 6 Wildfowl on the Roughshoot   78
 7 Pigeons on the Roughshoot   92
 8 Ground Game on the Roughshoot   106
 9 Deer and the Rifle on the Roughshoot   119
10 Predators, Traps and Trapping   135
11 The Dog on the Roughshoot   152
    Glossary   169
    Critical Bibliography   178

Preface and Acknowledgements

In 1957 I wrote a book entitled *The Roughshooter's Sport*, but a great deal has altered since those days of the gin trap, rearing under broody hens and subsidised cartridges for bona-fide pigeon shooters. There have been enormous changes in the past thirty years not only in shooting and shooting methods, but in the countryside and in agriculture. British-made guns are no longer the commonest nor, it should be said, always the best to be seen in the shooting field. Farmers are growing strange new crops and acre upon acre of new forestry is to be seen in many areas. Even the game on the shoot itself has changed in many ways. Certainly, methods of game rearing are greatly improved and simplified. The result is that this book is necessarily very different from its predecessor, to the extent that they do not even have a single paragraph in common.

It is always pointless to hark back to 'the good old days', if indeed they ever existed. It is necessary in my view to keep up with changes as they come along and adapt to them in order to survive. That is not to say that all new introductions are necessarily good. It is desirable to be selective. At the same time it is foolish to resist changes which are obvious improvements, or to attempt to hold back the tide of progress. For instance, four-wheel drive vehicles are something anyone in the countryside must welcome. Why get stuck in the mud when there is no need for it?

This book is intended to help people avoid getting stuck in the mire when it comes to roughshooting. It is intended as a guide to those who cannot afford the often astronomical costs of driven shooting, or who genuinely prefer, as I do, shooting over dogs with a few companions. For those who merely like the thought of shooting in the country, or for the farmer who wishes to improve his shooting, the book may also contain a few pointers.

The wildfowler, the pigeon shooter, the deer-stalker, the part-time keeper and the driven shot as well may find something of interest in these pages. The roughshooter today should, ideally, combine something of all these roles. But this book does not pretend to lay down hard and fast rules, for every roughshoot must differ, often very greatly, from the next. There are anyway always exceptions to almost every rule. On the other hand the roughshooter who approaches his sport on the lines indicated should enjoy it to the full. After forty years or more out almost every day with dog and gun I still enjoy each day and hope to go on doing so and learning something fresh on each outing. There is a limitless field of interest to anyone out in the countryside and prepared to keep their eyes open.

In conclusion, I must thank all those who have helped me with this book, particularly those responsible for the illustrations, notably Kathleen Blackie, Ian McCall, Patrick Douglas Hamilton, Christopher Wood and my wife, Evelyn. I must also thank all those who have helped me in other ways, in particular my various shooting partners over the years and the many dogs who have also taught me much about the country and the ways of wildlife, Max, Werra, Fred, Dan, Fiona, Bess, Gina, Kim, Lucy, Meg and the others. My heartfelt thanks must go once more to my wife, Evelyn, not only for putting up with the absurd hours I keep, but for, yet again, reading the typescript of yet another sporting book. For any errors or omissions, however, I am entirely responsible.

Michael Brander
July 1988

I

The Sporting Roughshoot

The Definition

The basic differences between a roughshoot and a driven shoot are
clear enough. A roughshoot does not have a full-time keeper, nor is
game reared and released on a large scale, nor is the game regularly
driven over the waiting guns by teams of professional beaters. Moors
may be seen as slightly different, in that game is seldom reared and
released on moorland, apart from possibly some partridges round
the edges. But if a moor is managed by a full-time keeper, or if the
grouse are regularly driven by means of professional beaters over
guns in butts, then it cannot be classified as a roughshoot. If there
is no keeper, or only a part-time keeper, and the grouse are usually
walked-up, or dogged, and not normally driven, then it clearly
qualifies as a moorland roughshoot.

Whether moorland or low ground, the size of a roughshoot may
vary from several thousand acres to a patch of fifty or so. Similarly,
of course, the size of a keepered driven shoot may also vary greatly
largely dependent on the terrain. The nature of the ground is obviously always of vital importance in any shoot. A small roughshoot
of fifty acres with a little wood and a stream and some mixed farmland
might provide much more sport throughout the year than five
hundred or even a thousand acres of bare windswept upland grassland shooting, or many hundred acres of dank and untended forestry.

Partnerships and syndicates

Few shoots of any size, whether keepered driven shoots or roughshoots, can stand being shot by more than eight, or at most ten,

guns. A roughshoot is probably best shared by a partnership of from
two to four guns, although sometimes syndicates of as many as
sixteen to twenty guns may take a shoot and split their shooting on
a voluntary basis, working a strict rota system whereby eight or ten
guns shoot, while the other eight or ten beat on alternate days
throughout the season. Rearing and keepering may also be carried
out on a similar voluntary shared basis. With modern simplified
methods of game rearing and feeding, large numbers of birds may
easily enough be reared and released even on a part-time basis. Such
a syndicate roughshoot, with a keen part-time keeper, or keepers,
may well provide better driven birds than many much more expensive but poorly-keepered and badly-managed driven shoots, or even
well-keepered shoots on less suitable ground. In such circumstances,
however, the shoot has then really ceased to be a roughshoot as such
and is more accurately described as a driven shoot run by amateurs.

Syndicates, to my mind, are seldom a particularly happy arrangement in any form of shooting, even if they are often the only solution
for driven shoots where the members are primarily required to share
the costs and otherwise need have little in common. The snag with
all syndicates of whatever size, on roughshoots, is that one seldom
finds six or eight, let alone sixteen or twenty, like-minded enthusiasts
all within equal distance of a shoot, who will work together without
friction. Inevitably one, or more, will constantly be complaining
about something, another will always be late, yet another may prove
an irritatingly selfish shot, or insist on bringing an uncontrolled dog,
and so on. With a partnership or from two to four, or at a pinch up
to six, members on a roughshoot it is possible to ensure that all are
like-minded and enjoy their sport with the same degree of enthusiastic participation.

Methods of Sharing a Roughshoot

It is only fair to add that the method mentioned above of sharing a
shoot between sixteen or more members of a syndicate can sometimes
work very successfully. There must, however, be an experienced
syndicate chairman, elected by vote, and his decisions must be
final. A rather less common method of sharing a roughshoot I have
encountered is basically a form of time sharing. In this case, six guns
share a Forestry Commission shoot on the Dorset borders and
take a day each week when they can shoot throughout the season.
Although in this case it works well since each is a professional man

who can only take a day, or half day, off each week, it is an unusual arrangement. Presumably the same principle could be extended to twelve guns with two guns sharing a day each week and shooting together, but there are obvious snags when too many people become involved in any such arrangements. Naturally to some extent the situation may be dictated by the finances involved. As a general rule, however, a smaller partnership of up to four, or six at the outside, is preferable to a large syndicate on a roughshoot.

Partnership Contributions

Inevitably there are those who do not have the time to spare, or possibly even the inclination, to go out and look after the roughshoot in the close season, yet who prefer roughshooting to driven game shooting. The answer for such people is to join together if they can with keener, or less fully occupied, friends and come to some mutually satisfactory agreement. If one partner gives his time, it is only reasonable that the other should provide a comparable financial commitment. Alternatively, some members of a partnership may provide financial backing in lieu of their time to pay towards rent, or feed, or other essentials, while other members of the partnership may provide their own special expertise. One may be an excellent and dedicated trapper, another an expert hide builder and decoy artist, a third a first rate hand at rearing young birds with facilities for providing good feed hoppers, and so on. It is thus that a good partnership will function successfully on a roughshoot.

Annual Roughshooting

Another method sometimes favoured by roughshooters who have only a fortnight or so each year to spend on their sport is to join the many peripatetic guns who answer advertisements offering various forms of shooting annually. In this way they may obtain quite good roughshooting in various parts of the country, varying their ground each year if they so wish. On the other hand, they will obviously not have the ultimate satisfaction of managing the roughshoot themselves, nor have the pleasure of watching over their own ground during the close season and of steadily building it up into a worthwhile shoot on which they know each acre intimately and the game to be expected on it. That is the ultimate satisfaction obtained from roughshooting and it is inevitably denied to the peripatetic roughshooter.

The Hunting Element

If the members of a small partnership wish to organise a driven day now and then, they may each invite a guest and provide a beater or two, if they feel the shoot will stand it. In normal circumstances, however, they will probably shoot over their dogs, and an element of hunting will naturally be a part of the day, which is absent in driven shooting. On a moorland roughshoot especially, the dogs will have to range wide and find and point game if the roughshooters hope to have a successful bag. On low ground the dogs will also have to be reliable hunters to ensure that game is not missed. If they are working out of range of the guns they must still point and hold the game, otherwise they must only find the game and push it up within range of the guns. Either way, they must be reliable hunters to ensure that game is not missed. There should always be a strong element of hunting in roughshooting which does not exist in driven shooting, except to a limited degree on the management and keepering sides.

The Organisation

The organiser of driven shooting is mainly concerned with presenting a succession of high birds over the guns to test their shooting skills to the utmost. Within reason, the more game over the guns the better. The roughshooter is less concerned with the quantity of game than with variety, with watching his dogs hunting their ground, with understanding and observing the ways of the wildlife on the ground, and only finally with presenting a challenging shot – although this too should always be one of his aims. In that his shots may often be taken while on the move over rough ground at game appearing unexpectedly from all angles, his sport is seldom comparable with driven shooting, but even if very different it may frequently be quite as difficult and every bit as satisfying.

In driven shooting the object should always be to kill each bird cleanly and well. In roughshooting the intention will also be to kill cleanly and well, but in the event of a bird being wounded, the roughshooter should be able to spend as long as is required to ensure that bird is retrieved and despatched, while the driven shooter must rely on others to retrieve his game. The roughshooter will be able to shoot selectively, taking care to kill off the old birds early in the season in order to split up the coveys and provide more sport throughout the season. This should have the effect of producing more birds in the ensuing year as well, since the young birds will not be driven off the territory by the older birds and there should be more birds breeding on the ground.

The roughshooter may also make a point of preserving hen birds where necessary since he is acting as his own game preserver and take care to shoot any crows, magpies or mink and similar predators which may be encountered, even if this may disturb game nearby. In general, the driven game shot will restrict his shooting to game only, since to do otherwise may be to disrupt a drive or miss a shot at game, and to incur the displeasure of his host or the organiser of the day.

Successful Days

Although it is almost always possible to have a driven day on a roughshoot, or, for that matter, for a few guns to have what amounts to a roughshooting day on part of a driven shoot, in general the two sports are very different. A successful day's roughshooting may mean the roughshooters walking over several miles' hard going. It may end with them having only fired half a dozen shots apiece, if that, but with six or eight varieties of game in the bag. Although making up only a dozen or so head, each of those will probably be satisfactorily engraved in the memory for years to come. During a successful day's driven shooting the guns may only walk a few hundred yards in all between drives. The bag may consist of several hundred birds, mostly of the same species. If the day has been well organised, the guns will have enjoyed their shooting and their skill will have been tested to the full, but as can be seen there is very little comparison between the two forms of sport.

Knowledge of the Sport

This is in no way to decry either form of sport for they are entirely complementary and may often take place satisfactorily at different times on the same ground, or adjacent to each other. The keen sporting roughshooter should always be prepared to accept an invitation to shoot driven game or to pick up with his dogs or to beat, by way of variety, if he has the opportunity to do so. He should enjoy his day and may always learn something in the process. Similarly, the keen driven game shot should always be prepared to accept the chance of a day's roughshooting to keep himself in trim and to exercise his dogs if nothing more. It is always interesting to shoot on different ground and it can also be a very useful experience to watch others shooting for a change. The experienced sportsman will accept any opportunities for roughshooting or for driven shooting and will be prepared to take his place amongst the beaters or pickers-up whenever he is invited to do so, knowing that he is likely to have an enjoyable day's sport.

Knowledge of the Ground

During the driven day the amateur, or professional, pickers-up and the beaters should have had the pleasure of seeing some good shooting, as well as watching their dogs work successfully and knowing they have contributed to the day's success. The keeper and shoot manager will also have had the satisfaction of using their knowledge of the ground and the ways of the wildlife on it to the full to present the birds at their best over the guns. The roughshooter who has a sound knowledge of his ground and of the game on it will experience the satisfaction of all those concerned in the driven day, thus gaining the best of both worlds, even if on a very much smaller scale.

When roughshooting with only a few guns, the object should be to use the acquired knowledge of the ground and the likely movements and reactions of the wild game on it to provide the best shooting available. Similar methods to those used by the keeper and beaters on a driven day may often be used on a roughshoot. The same principles of moving game as and where required may be employed on a smaller scale, depending on the size of the roughshoot, the amount of game present and the number of people involved. When working with only three or four guns, or even less, the problem of moving game and presenting it successfully can obviously be much greater than with larger numbers of guns and beaters available. Much has to depend on the ground, but basically even more depends on the knowledge the roughshooter has of it and of the game and its likely reactions.

Borderline Shoots

Some shoots, of course, must be close to the borderline and may even vary from season to season. One example is a 2,500 acres shoot to which I was frequently invited some years ago by the owner who employed two full-time keepers and reared between 2,000–3,000 pheasants a year. When the owner died the effect of death duties was that only one full-time keeper was employed and the shoot was let to a syndicate of eight businessmen. Since I knew several of them I was still invited to shoot on occasions and found the standard of birds and the bags little changed. Finally the old keeper retired and the owner decided not to replace him. The syndicate then employed a part-time keeper and a lad and with their help reared 1,500 birds. Since they continued to employ beaters and shoot only driven birds as before, the shoot still did not qualify as a roughshoot, but had they ceased to employ beaters and organise regular driven days it would then, by definition, have become a roughshoot. The difference between the two is often narrow enough.

With the original owner I often had what amounted to rough-shooting days with only two or three of us wandering round the rougher outskirts of one side and shooting over dogs. The ground in question lends itself quite effectively to running as a driven shoot in the main area with a roughshoot of some four hundred acres on one edge, which it is almost impossible to drive effectively. It is in fact a good example of a shoot which, although partially laid out for driven shooting over around eight guns, also has one part which is ideal for roughshooting with two or three guns only. As in this instance, the terrain often dictates how an area is shot, for some ground is obviously useless for driven shooting yet may well provide excellent sport for one or two guns and dogs.

The Ground

Most large estates appreciate that the ground dictates the shooting and on a large area the policy is usually adopted of dividing it into different shoots to suit the terrain. Thus a large estate may well have several shoots running concurrently on the ground adjacent to each other. These are usually all keepered and organised driven shoots to obtain the maximum financial return from the shooting. It can happen, however, that it sometimes pays to set aside some of the ground as a roughshoot, where for one reason or another it does not lend itself to driven shooting. A keeper may, or may not, oversee such ground on a full or part-time basis and game may, or may not, be released on it depending on which methods the estate favours as providing the best financial return.

For example, on one 10,000 acre estate in the Lowlands of Scotland where I was asked to advise on the shooting, there was just such a tract of very wild overgrown land, pitted with narrow ravines and unsuitable for driving, which was close to the edge of a mining town and from which the local poachers launched what amounted to organised raids on the main shoot. Fortunately there was a simple solution. The local police were keen on shooting, and roughshooting in that area of large estates was not readily available. By offering them top wages for beating as well as this patch of 400 acres as a roughshoot the problem of persistent poaching was very soon brought under control. Thereafter the main driven shoot flourished as never before.

Finding a Roughshoot

The question of how to find a roughshoot is one that arises whenever the subject is mentioned. This is one of the occasions when the dictum that all men are equal is proved totally untrue. The man who lives in a large city is at a considerable disadvantage compared with the man who lives in the country, or in a small town or village. The only sound advice that can be given to the city dweller who wants a roughshoot is to study the advertisements to be found in most sporting magazines advertising roughshooting and follow them up until he finds something worthwhile. Alternatively, if he has friends in the country or a connection, however tenuous, with some special area, he might do well to start from there.

With the help of people on the spot it is usually easier to find something suitable. The best roughshooting is seldom advertised. Another possibility may be to join the nearest roughshooting, or wildfowling, club. These are almost all affiliated to the British Association for Shooting and Conservation, B.A.S.C., whose headquarters are at Marford Mill, Rossett, Wrexham, Clwyd, LL12 OHL. A letter to them applying for membership, which in any event provides built-in insurance against shooting accidents and many other advantages, could be the first step in putting the complete novice roughshooter in touch with people who may be able to help him.

In that within reason any piece of ground is a potential roughshoot it is really impossible to provide any ready answer as to where to find roughshooting. It must depend on so many unknown and varied factors such as the time each individual has available or is prepared to spare for his sport, as well as the obvious question of where he lives and the standard of shooting he requires. Presuming that the individual has plenty of time available and is prepared to keep trying on the lines indicated above, despite many disappointments the chances are that he will eventually find some suitable shooting.

The Forestry Commission Shoot

The Forestry Commission is still one of the largest landowners in the country and has many areas of ground available for shooting, some of which can provide very good sport indeed. Equally it must be admitted that it also has many areas of ground which are simply not worth bothering about. The difficulty is that their system of competitive tendering for leases and of leasing to the highest bidder can make bidding for their shoots something of a lottery. Once a shoot has been acquired, however, the successful bidder is usually given first refusal subsequently when the lease comes up for renewal. The difficulty is that unless the potential roughshooter knows a good deal about the growth of trees and forestry procedures he may well find that he is bidding a high price for the lease of land which, with young trees growing steadily, soon becomes no use for shooting and merely a haven for predators.

On the other hand, if good relations are maintained with the Forestry Commission Ranger in charge of a local area, what may at first sight seem a poor shoot initially may well be greatly improved with his co-operation. A friend of mine with just such a shoot in Thetford Chase asked me to advise him and help him to organise it. It consisted of two 200 acre farms surrounded by over 500 acres of forestry in various blocks. Fortunately good relations were established with the Ranger in charge of the area. By persuading the Forestry Commission to agree to clear fell 100 acres of mature trees between the two farms, what had been some rather indifferent roughshooting was transformed into a very satisfactory driven shoot. Yet this was in an area where any form of shooting is hard to obtain.

Unlikely Ground

Naturally enough, as in the case just quoted, it can be very much more difficult to obtain roughshooting in some areas than in others and it was an undoubted advantage from my friend's viewpoint that he lived on the ground. Near to large towns especially, understandably enough, roughshooting is generally hard to obtain. The land is either used for other purposes, or else is let to syndicates for driven shooting. Yet, even here, often in the most unlikely places, the diligent searcher may still find places where a roughshoot may be successfully built up on apparently unpromising ground.

It is indeed often the seemingly least promising ground which turns out to be most suitable for roughshooting. Sewage works, abandoned quarries, old bing heaps, deserted gravel pits, overgrown railway sidings, small patches of scrub forest, or undrained bog, or old open cast workings and similar ground which has been ignored by others may provide a roughshoot of anything from fifty acres upwards. Unfortunately these sort of waste spaces are becoming increasingly rare with the widespread desire to beautify the countryside, but they are still to be found here and there and can often be well worth converting into a roughshoot.

The Farm Shoot

Best of all, of course, is to find a farm on which the farmer is prepared to co-operate in building up a good roughshoot. It is often difficult to find this combination close at hand, and it may be necessary to travel far afield to obtain it, but that is close to the ideal. With the co-operation of the man on the spot a great deal is possible.

During the three decades since the war farming has enjoyed one of its periodic booms. Accordingly roughshooting in particular has been hard to obtain since farmers have not felt the necessity to lease their land for sporting purposes, or have preferred merely to shoot it occasionally themselves. The situation has now changed greatly and farmers find themselves forced to diversify and seek other sources of income in order to survive. Since the agricultural depression of the 1870s it has been the case that when farming was in decline shooting has increased in popularity and general availability, encouraged by the farmers themselves. When agriculture has been booming, as in recent years, shooting has been harder to obtain since crops have been at a premium and farmers have not wished to bother about extraneous means of earning an income.

The Potential

One feature which almost all farms have in common, although many have ignored it in the boom years, is a basic potential for rough-shooting. Even if the ground is seemingly bare, with few hedges or cover, something can usually be achieved in the way of shooting. With the assistance of the farmer there is always some potential on the most unlikely looking ground, even if it only consists of a few rabbits and pigeons along with the occasional covey of partridges.

For the keen roughshooter with an eye to the future this may well be enough on which to build, since with the farmer's help and approval many quite far-reaching alterations are feasible and what at first may be seemingly impossible ground can be turned with effort and enthusiasm into an interesting roughshoot. With the addition for instance of a little cover here and there, even if it only consists of a strip of rape along a hedgerow, or a small patch of conifers or fast growing shrubs, and by excavating a carefully sited flight pond, or erecting a couple of well placed treetop platforms for pigeon flighting, what might have appeared somewhat unpromising land may be transformed surprisingly quickly into a very satisfying and varied roughshoot.

The Game Conservancy

Once a suitable prospective shoot has been found and a satisfactory lease has been signed transferring the shooting rights for a reasonable period of years (certainly not less than three and preferably five with an option to continue), it is a sound plan to call on the services of the Game Conservancy. The Game Conservancy with its head-quarters at Fordingbridge, Hampshire, has a team of professional advisers who cover the country. For a very reasonable fee they will spend a day on the ground and report on their findings with detailed advice on how best to improve the shooting. With their vast experi-ence this is a service well worth consideration by any size of shoot and, set against the likely improvement in the shooting, the fee may be seen as a very sound investment.

EASE OF ACCESS

The question of whether to choose an indifferent area of rough-shooting near at hand or a better shoot further afield is always a difficult one which each individual must decide for himself after balancing the advantages against the disadvantages. In general it is usually best to go for the closer shoot. Ease of access always makes it simpler to keep a close eye on everything connected with improving the shoot in addition to keeping down the overall travelling costs. These can become a very considerable factor, more especially if the shoot is to be visited daily, or at least several times each week during the breeding season for instance.

A Presence on the Shoot

The shoot which has someone present on it who is likely to be helpful is generally to be preferred even to a more promising area which has no-one reliable resident nearby who may be of assistance when required. Such a person need not be required to do more than telephone to say that they have heard shots being fired on the ground, or that they saw a fox passing over such and such a field. The mere presence of someone reliable on the shoot is an enormous asset to any roughshooter who does not live on the ground himself. By inviting the tenant farmer, the farm manager, the foreman, or others on the spot to shoot and gaining their interest and support, even if only by presenting them with a brace of pheasants or other game from time to time, the roughshooter is likely to find his sport greatly improved. The ideal situation, of course, is when the roughshooter, or one of the partnership, lives on the ground himself and is always available to keep an eye on matters.

YEAR ROUND INTEREST

The essence of roughshooting is the business of looking after the shoot and the game on it throughout the year so as to obtain the most enjoyable sport that the ground can provide. In his efforts to ensure the best sport available from the ground, the keen rough-shooter should obtain as great enjoyment and satisfaction at times during the close season as he is likely to obtain during the peak months of the shooting season itself. It is in maintaining a year-round interest in the ground and all the circumstances affecting it – the weather, the crops, the animals and birds, extending to the people connected with it as well as the interaction of all these – that the roughshooter will often find his greatest satisfaction. Knowing the ground, the game and everything affecting it provides him with a satisfying stake in the countryside itself.

The Variety of the Roughshoot

From the foregoing it will be seen that to try to define a roughshoot is as impossible as it is to define a piece of string. Firstly, the shoot itself may vary in size and location. It may also vary in the game likely to be encountered and the ease with which it may be altered or improved. The numbers involved in shooting it may differ as well as the methods employed to run it. Hardly any two roughshoots are likely to pose similar problems or provide precisely similar sport. That in itself is one of the pleasures to be obtained from roughshooting.

The roughshooter should naturally view any piece of ground with an eye to improving it as much as possible. Most shoots, or prospective shoots, will have a tendency to prove attractive to one or more of the gamebirds normally encountered in the British Isles. It is up to the roughshooter to consider how the ground may be keepered and improved and the various gamebirds encouraged to thrive on it.

Perhaps one shoot is more obviously attractive to wildfowl, with boggy patches for snipe, woodcock and pheasant, while another is more clearly suitable for partridges, pigeons and groundgame. Yet another may obviously be a moorland shoot with grouse and even blackgame available. Whether other game can be encouraged on each of these different shoots is one of the problems facing the roughshooter. Whereas the driven game shot is generally interested primarily in the quantities of game available and the degree of challenge involved in the shooting, the confirmed roughshooter is likely to be more interested in the variety of the day's bag rather than the quantity, although the challenging quality of the shooting should also interest him, since no-one wishes just to shoot birds up the backside. The aim of the roughshooter should be to ensure that his shooting is never dull.

The Observation of Wildlife

It is one of the many pleasures of roughshooting that there are always likely to be moments of interest in an otherwise blank day. It is in the satisfaction of hunting with dog and gun that the roughshooter obtains a large part of his enjoyment. A brace of hen pheasants spared to breed for the coming season, or a mating pair of partridges left deliberately towards the end of the season, may provide as much inward satisfaction as a rocketing high bird killed in full-flight as it cleared the treetops in a mid-November shoot. There are almost always rabbits and pigeons, both in and out of season, to rely on as standbys, but the real satisfaction of a roughshoot is often found in observing the ways of the wildlife on it as much as in the shooting.

Watching the changing seasons on the shoot can be full of interest. Spotting the young woodcock, like apricot balls of fluff, gathered round and under the parent bird, visible only by the enormous liquid eye in a patch of cover, or listening to the sound of geese passing overhead while waiting for the duck to flight in the darkening shades of the evening, or seeing the young ducklings in spring swimming busily downstream in line behind their proud mother, or following the tracks of the hunting fox in the snow, or spying the hare in the stubble leaping sharply sideways into his form soon after dawn, while the roe filter gradually back to the woods, or catching sight of an old badger waddling purposefully back to his earth, all these are part of the roughshooter's year and make up an important part of his sport and enjoyment. The shooting at times becomes a very minor part of the proceedings.

The Rifle on the Roughshoot

The introduction of a rifle to enhance the sport, on the other hand, brings a fresh dimension to the roughshoot. Even a powerful .22 air rifle can be a useful weapon on the roughshoot at times, although a .22 rifle with, or without, a sound modifier is greatly preferable. With such a weapon it is possible to shoot not only those wily out-of-range old crows and magpies, but also ground predators such as mink and foxes. On occasion squirrels and groundgame may also be stalked and shot with the .22. Using a heavier calibre, such as a .243 or .270, deer may be still-hunted in the woods, or stalked in the open, for there are few parts of the country where deer of one kind or another are not to be found and thus the roughshooter's horizons may be expanded and further good sport obtained throughout the year.

Time Required

Whether shooting deer with a rifle, or trapping predators, the rough-shooter who so wishes will find his time very fully occupied throughout the year. Like anyone intimately connected with the countryside and the land he will soon appreciate that results cannot always be expected within days, months or sometimes even years. The sporting roughshoot should be a full-time occupation for the keen rough-shooter. The annual cycle of spring, summer, autumn and winter each produces its special problems, its attractions and its work. Overseeing the care of the wildlife, and not merely the game, on the sporting roughshoot, should take up all the time that the rough-shooter can spare.

The Trap Round

Attention to a trap round, as any gamekeeper will testify, can be a full-time occupation. Knowledge of where the predators on the shoot are likely to be found as well as keeping them under control is just as important to the wildlife of the hedgerow and copse, to the small songbirds and to beasts such as voles and fieldmice on which many predators exist in the natural course of events. To maintain an even balance of the natural wildlife population is part of the rough-shooter's task if he is to achieve a good sporting roughshoot. Organising a trap round is one of the ancillary aspects of his sport from which the roughshooter may gain considerable satisfaction as well as learning a great deal.

Game Rearing

Rearing even a small number of birds to release on the shoot, whether wildfowl, partridges or pheasants, can be of considerable interest as well as very time-consuming. Watching the youngsters hatch out from the eggs into feathered balls of fluff, then mature into gawky half-grown birds and finally into sleek mature adults is a very reward-ing process. Learning to know the birds, watching them at feeding times, getting to know their various territories and their individual colourings, markings and characteristics brings yet another dimension into the shooting. The roughshooter game preserver will inevitably find he has a much closer relationship with birds he has reared and released himself.

Knowledge of the area over which he has control should extend to the territories not only of the gamebirds and smaller mammals, but also the larger ones, which may cover areas far beyond the bounds of the roughshoot itself, for instance, deer and foxes and even hares. As his knowledge of the ground grows he will find that animals such as mink or even stoats and weasels, as well as birds from crows and magpies to buzzards and hawks, may also cover far greater areas, including the roughshoot, than he had appreciated. By following their movements and working out the causes – the cutting of crops, the flooding of riverbank fields, the changes in the weather and so on – he can in the course of time learn to anticipate what is likely to happen.

The Roughshooter Naturalist

It is in his role as a naturalist and conservationist that the roughshooter will find much of interest. He will come to appreciate that each bird and beast has its own place in the overall picture, the pecking order of Nature. He will find that just as the master roebuck may keep the young bucks off his territory, thus limiting the damage caused to the trees, so foxes, stoats and other predators tend to have their own areas clearly defined. Gradually the pieces of the puzzle will begin to fit into place and will become relatively clear to him so that he will know where each territory begins and ends. In certain meeting places, or main roads as it were, a trap set will almost always take its toll of the unwary. Wherever there is evidence of too much damage being caused by predators, or by over-population, it becomes a matter of course to try to attend to it to even the balance.

Observation

In the spring, tracks in the mud, or in the winter, in the snow, will often reveal much of the movements of the local wildlife populations. Long hours spent in hides, at ground or at treetop level, watching the movements of wildlife will never be wasted. Binoculars and patience can reap dividends on any roughshoot and it is as a naturalist observer that sometimes as much satisfaction can be obtained from the sporting roughshoot as from the actual shooting, if not more.

Indeed it would not be going too far to say that some of the experienced roughshooter's most satisfying moments may well have been almost totally unconnected with shooting, although only experienced as a result of his enthusiasm for his roughshoot. Watching the roe doe and the buck in their mad courtship chases and later the doe playing with her young, seeing blackgame at their leck, serious and courtly, absurdly like eighteenth-century dancers bobbing and bowing in a quadrille, or watching two young cock pheasants facing up to each other in earnest heedless of the proximity of observers, or a group of hares in March playing tag and follow-my-leader in a broad stubble field, all these and many more such spectacles are the reward of the roughshooter engaged in building up the sporting roughshoot.

Understanding the Roughshoot

Until he has attained a full understanding of his roughshoot and the animals and birds which live on it, the roughshooter will not have the deep satisfaction which he should ultimately achieve when walking round the ground. This is not to say that he may not have excellent sport and gain enormous pleasure while he is learning the various secrets of the ground. It is always an exciting business walking round during the various seasons of the year and seeing fresh traces of the birds and beasts which live there, thus building up an overall picture of the wildlife on it.

Finally, the complete living mosaic becomes fully understood and appreciated. It is in establishing such an understanding of the ground over which he shoots and of the wildlife on it that the roughshooter gains the maximum return from his sport. The more he puts into his sport the more he is likely to gain in return. It is only when the roughshooter has achieved this complete identification with his ground and the wildlife on it that he will experience the maximum pleasure from the sporting roughshoot.

2

Requisites and Prerequisites

The equipment required for the roughshoot is best considered on two levels. There are primarily the items required by the rough-shooter personally and there are on the other hand those which will be required on the roughshoot itself. It is also necessary to remember those items which are required before it is possible even to consider roughshooting. The principal requisites and prerequisites are as follows:

PERSONAL PREREQUISITES

Shotgun Certificate

It is illegal to own a shotgun without a Shotgun Certificate issued by the police. Before buying a shotgun it is essential that the would-be roughshooter applies at his local police station for a Shotgun Certificate. Unless he is considered an unsuitable person owing to a history of mental illness or having been in prison, the police should have no reason for not approving the holding of a Shotgun Certificate on payment of an initial fee of £12, renewable at three year intervals on payment of a further fee of £8 for each renewal. This certificate entitles the holder to buy any number of shotguns, either from a licensed dealer, or privately. The only restrictions are that the shotgun barrels must be over twenty-four inches in length and they must not be pump action guns. Each should be proved with the current proof marks of the Birmingham Proof House or they may not be legally sold.

Firearms Certificate

If the roughshooter wishes to use a pump action shot gun, a .22, or heavier calibre rifle on his ground he must first apply for a Firearms Certificate. He will have to show good reason for requiring them and if he is not a landowner will have to produce written permission from the landowner over whose ground he is intending to use them. The police must be assured that the owner of a Firearms Certificate is a suitable person to own a rifle and has suitable premises where it will be kept in a safe place under lock and key. Those with a history of mental illness, alcoholism or who have been in prison are likely to be refused a Certificate. Subject to a Firearms Certificate being issued and payment of the initial fee of £25, with a renewal fee of £20 at three year intervals, or when it is desired to alter the particulars on it, a rifle and the appropriate supplies of ammunition may then be purchased.

Game Licence

Neither possession of a Shotgun Certificate, nor of a Firearms Certificate entitles the holder to shoot game. The holders of such Licences may shoot pigeons, rabbits, squirrels and most predators, but they may not shoot either game or deer without a Game Licence.

Possession of a Game Licence entitles the holder to demand the production of a Game Licence from anyone he may encounter shooting game. The Game Licence for a full year costs £6 and is renewable annually. Paradoxically it is not necessary to have a Shotgun Certificate or Firearms Certificate to have a Game Licence.

Shooting Lease

Although satisfactory shooting can sometimes be obtained simply by verbal agreement on a year to year basis, this is not generally to be recommended. A suitable shooting lease should outline the boundaries, detail what may be shot and what rights the shooting tenant may be allowed regarding erecting platforms, hides, or digging flight ponds, with agreement on points such as establishing cover, either temporary or permanent. It should contain exact details of payments due and of permission to rear and release birds. Any liabilities for roadmaking, fence building and so on should be included. It should be for at least a minimum three year agreement with an option to continue.

Map

A large-scale map of at least one inch to the mile showing not only the area of the shoot with the boundaries clearly marked, but also showing the surrounding area, is an important necessity. Several copies of it will be helpful. On these the roughshooter can mark where game is reared and released, where game is seen and shot, and similar details. He can note likely flight lines dictated by contours and forestry, and the siting of treetop platforms and ground level hides. Neighbouring crops and likely sources of feed or attractive areas for game should also be included. Any particular favourite haunts for predators, such as fox earths, should be marked. Warrens, pigeon roosting woods and similar factors affecting the shooting should likewise be noted. Any trap-lines set, plus the success ratios may also be included. Such maps will prove of very practical value on the shoot. At the end of each year the appropriate maps should be filed in the Game Records.

Game Records

A gamebook, Record or Register of each day spent on the shoot, whether game is shot or not, detailing such points as weather, game seen, evidence of predators, shots fired, or action taken, any trapping or feeding done and all other significant observations will make a valuable record over the years. It is surprising how often conditions are seen to repeat each other in a noticeable cycle over a period of time. This need not be a specially bound volume. In fact a loose-leaf folder has considerable advantages in that the leaves may be taken out and inserted at will if mistakes are made and it is necessary to correct them or add something at a later date. Combined with copies of an annotated map inserted at intervals, these Game registers can be a very valuable guide as to the progress of the shoot. Properly kept, such a record should be very much more than just a dull diary of each day and in later years may provide many pleasant memories as well as valuable information for subsequent roughshooters.

Insurance

It is usually part of any lease agreement that the roughshooter will be insured against liability to any third party resulting from any shooting accident. The roughshooter will also wish to be insured against damage to his gun or equipment. The former is automatic if the roughshooter is a member of B.A.S.C. and the latter is probably included under a normal comprehensive household insurance policy, but it is as well to check this. In any event, insurance is a point that should not be overlooked.

PERSONAL REQUISITES

Shotgun

Whatever else the roughshooter may dispense with he will need at least one shotgun. The choice of a shotgun is a very personal matter, like the choice of underwear. Whether you like to mortify the flesh by wearing sackcloth and ashes or whether you prefer silk from Kashmir is up to you. The choice of a gun must vary as widely with each individual. For instance one man may prefer the sighting plane provided by the top rib of an over and under whereas another may prefer a side by side double barrel. Finances may affect the issue, but basically it is a matter for individual choice. A few guidelines may be laid down, but that is about all.

The roughshooter definitely does not require a valuable gun by a well-known gunmaker. His gun should be robust and able to stand up to harsh treatment, scratches from thick undergrowth, or being left in the back of cars with several dogs and gamebags thrust unceremoniously on top of it, and so on. It is probably best bored cylinder and half choke, but again everyone will have their own choice on that. If finances are really strained a single barrel may be used, but naturally this tends to limit the opportunities for sport somewhat. Unlike driven shooting, there is seldom anything gained by being able to reload rapidly so that an ejector is no great advantage on the roughshoot.

Sadly guns by English makers are largely priced out of the market today. Good Spanish, Italian and even Russian guns, either side by side, ejectors and non-ejectors, or over and unders if preferred, can be obtained quite cheaply. There is almost an embarrassment of choice today and the novice will be well-advised to put himself in the hands of a reliable gunmaker and be guided by him. It is in all good gunmakers's own interests to see that a customer is satisfied, since if he is then the chances are that he will come back to buy cartridges and other equipment, even possibly another gun, or guns. In passing it is worth pointing out that collecting guns can very easily become a vice and there is really no need for the roughshooter to have more than one gun. It should be regarded as a working tool and cared for as such rather than seen as a thing of beauty to be admired for the quality and the workmanship that has gone into it.

What gauge of shotgun, whether 12, 16 or 20 bore is chosen, is again a matter of personal preference. It is argued that 20-bores should not be owned along with 12-bores since a 20-bore cartridge may slip inside a 12-bore gun and allow a 12-bore cartridge to be inserted on top, resulting in the gun bursting if it is then fired. Such an accident is unlikely, but has been known. The advantages of the smaller gauges are mainly lightness. The advantage of the 12-bore is that cartridges are always readily available whereas with other bores this is not always the case.

There will always be those, especially those with money to spare or enthusiasm drowning their common sense, who will insist on having a 12-bore side by side for roughshooting as well as a 12-bore under and over for clay pigeon shooting, with possibly a 28-bore or a .410 for shooting rabbits when ferreting. This, of course, is the thin end of the wedge. It is not long before a fully-choked 12-bore with three inch barrels is acquired for wildfowling. Then a specially good side by side 12-bore is also required for occasional driven days. It may even be that a matched pair of best sidelocks are required for days at driven grouse when a loader is required. The collecting bug comes in many forms and is to be avoided as far as possible.

There may still be some who recommend a pump gun or semi-automatic for roughshooting. It is perhaps unnecessary to comment unduly. A Firearms Certificate is required to own one, while it is illegal to use a semi-automatic in most circumstances with more than two cartridges. The worst feature of both these types of shotgun is that it is impossible to tell simply by looking at them whether they are loaded or unloaded. Unlike a normal shotgun the action cannot be broken to demonstrate publicly that the barrels are unloaded. It is thus possible to forget to unload, only to find that you have a loaded gun in a car or other confined space, which could be lethal. This is enough to condemn them to my mind, but everyone has to make their own decisions and there are undoubtedly those who will stand by these weapons if only out of sheer obstinacy.

A .410 may be useful at times when a 12-bore might prove too powerful at close range, as for instance when ferreting and shooting rabbits bolting from burrows. A 12-bore at close range would reduce them to soup, whereas a .410 would kill them neatly. A .410 adaptor which slips into the chamber of a 12-bore is an inexpensive way of adapting a 12-bore to fire .410 cartridges. It can be carried in the pocket and used when required. Either a .410 or adaptors may be a useful addition to the roughshooter's armoury in addition to his choice of 12-bore.

Cartridges and Cartridge Extractor

There can be no hard and fast rule as to which cartridges to use. Some shots will advocate using No. 6 shot throughout the year, others No. 5, or No. 7. A great deal depends on the shooting involved, but even more on the shotgun and the man using it. If the cartridges suit the gun and provide a good pattern that is half the battle. If the shooter has confidence in his cartridges that is even more important. Confidence is all-important and if for some reason a batch of cartridges proves defective it can be most demoralising.

If a cartridge should jam in the breech due to a swollen or damaged case there can be few more annoying things than being unable to extract it. This may happen only once or twice in a shooting lifetime, but a day can be spoiled as a result. It is always worth having an extractor fastened to a cartridge bag or cartridge belt for use in such an emergency.

Rifle

A .22 is definitely a useful part of the roughshooter's armoury. A bolt action .22 with telescopic sight can be very useful for various predators on the roughshoot. Mink, foxes, crows and magpies can all be stalked and shot. The addition of a silencer, or sound modifier, may be considered well worthwhile. When shooting groundgame especially, there is often a chance of a second or even a third shot if a silencer is used before the quarry is alerted.

If deer are to be shot a heavier calibre, such as .243 is essential. It is illegal to shoot deer with a .22. In Scotland a .222 is still legal for deer, although not in England. In fact for deer such as Muntjac or the rarer Chinese Water deer a .222 would undoubtedly be the most suitable weapon since a .243 is almost too powerful for these deer, which are considerably smaller than roe deer. It is time that similar laws on deer were instituted in both England and Scotland. The .222 is considerably heavier than the .22, but nothing like as heavy as the .243. It is decidedly not suitable for any deer larger than roe. A .243 is suitable for most deer but may be regarded by some as too light for red deer. A .270 is regarded by some as the most suitable all-round rifle, but is undoubtedly too heavy for smaller deer such as Muntjac and Chinese Water deer, while many regard it as liable to damage the carcase of a roe unduly.

Air Rifle

A powerful air rifle may sometimes be used instead of a .22 and this can also be a useful addition to the roughshooter's armoury, being a silent means of killing crows and magpies at quite reasonable ranges. While some are powerful enough for groundgame and squirrels at fairly close range, they are not suitable for foxes. They do not have the killing power of a .22, but there are times when they can prove very effective. They do have the advantage that no Licence is required if the buyer is over the age of seventeen. They should be regarded, however, as very much at the bottom end of the roughshooter's armoury.

OTHER REQUISITES

Gamebag

This should be roomy enough to take at least a pair of large hares at a pinch. That will probably be as much as most people want to carry any distance and anything more will seriously unbalance the roughshooter and is bound to affect his shooting adversely. (In passing, it is surprising how many hares are missed at the start of a long day's roughshooting.) The commonest type of gamebag in Britain has a broad carrying band and a washable interior, with a leather bound net strung on the outside. They come in various sizes and the largest will take three or four hares inside and probably two outside. Six hares will unbalance anyone and after half a mile or so even the strongest and toughest are likely to lose interest in shooting much more.

Useful outer waistcoat type gamebags, commonly seen in the U.S.A., which can be put on over the shooting coat and which have a back game pocket that can hold a considerable amount of game are also quite good, but usually have the disadvantage that after the first game has been slipped into them it becomes necessary to take them off each time it is wished to insert more game, or else get a companion to load it up. Another point with some of this type of gamebag-waistcoat is that game can sometimes fall out unnoticed when crossing obstacles such as fences or dykes. The same, however, is true of almost any gamebag towards the end of a successful day when it is well filled. The advantage of the traditional British type first noted is that they have straps enabling the bag to be firmly closed when it is full to prevent game being lost in this manner. The advantage of the waistcoat type bag is that the weight of the game tends to be more evenly balanced so that the roughshooter is able to shoot more comfortably, without feeling disconcertingly one-sided. The traditional type has one other advantage over the waistcoat type in that it can be readily unfastened or slipped off and used as a convenient protection for crossing over a barbed wire fence and protecting the clothes from rips. To use a waistcoat type gamebag in the same way necessitates undoing it and slipping both arms out of it – very nearly the same process as taking off a coat. Even then it is not such a robust protection and is liable to rip. On most counts the traditional type is preferable, but the waistcoat variety has advantages of its own, not least on the moor when it can be a light-weight protection against passing showers or provide extra warmth on cold days. Some even have a detachable lining for this purpose. On the whole this is simply a matter of personal choice. There are those who prefer to carry their game attached to their belts, but this tends to make the clothing unnecessarily bloody.

Cartridge Belt

A cartridge belt for around twenty-five cartridges is best made of solid leather loops into which the cartridges fit neatly. Spring clips holding the cartridges are an anathema as they will catch in obstructions, such as twigs and bushes, when moving through cover and cartridges may readily be lost. Those with hooks, for carrying game or for attaching a dog lead, are undesirable as they catch in jackets if worn underneath the outer coat, or in twigs and bushes if worn outside the coat. If it is raining hard it is generally worth wearing the belt inside the coat to keep the cartridges dry, but otherwise for convenience sake it is preferable to wear the belt outside the shooting jacket. It is often best to keep half a dozen or so cartridges in reserve in an outer pocket and replenish these as often as required from the belt.

Cartridge Bag

This may or may not be felt necessary. They are really more useful on a driven day but can be very handy when, for instance, flighting pigeons or duck. They may hold anything from 50 to 250 cartridges. Probably the commonest size holds 150 cartridges. Made of leather or canvas, they should have a good stiffened leather-bound opening so that the hand can readily reach in for additional cartridges without fumbling.

Gun Sleeve

This may be of canvas or leather. It may simply open with a strap at one end, or have a zip running the full length. It may be lined with kapok or wool and should have a leather sling to allow it to be carried over the shoulder. The type made of leather with a heavy-duty full-length zip and lined with wool are generally preferable to, if more bulky than, the canvas variety. It has the advantage that it can be fully opened and dried out if the gun has had to be put away wet, and it also prevents the gun being damaged if the case should knock against a car door or similar obstacle. On the other hand, the canvas case is readily stowed away in a pocket or gamebag and is very useful for carrying the gun when it is necessary to carry other equipment as well. It does not, however, provide the degree of protection from damage that the other affords. Furthermore, it is no great protection against rain and will require very thorough drying out should it become wet. Gun sleeves may, of course, be used for both shotguns and rifles.

Boots

These are perhaps the most important item of gear. The boots should fit comfortably and should be tough and preferably waterproof. It should be possible to hike twenty miles in them over tough going without getting wet feet, blisters, or losing their grip. They should also be as light as possible. Good ankle boots laced up comfortably are probably the best answer. Rubber wellington boots, whether green or black, are not comfortable for long distance walking and totally unsuited to moorland, or for that matter much low ground. On the other hand, on a low ground boggy shoot or where there are small streams or shallow rivers to be crossed at intervals, a pair of calf-length rubber boots may well be the most sensible thing to wear since otherwise the legs and feet may end up soaking wet. There may even be places such as boggy ground or tidal estuaries on the foreshore, where thigh-length waders are the sensible garb. There are people prepared to walk all day in these in boggy moorland where snipe and duck may be found, but there are those who feel it is probably just as well to get wet and walk more easily.

Headgear

The hat or cap should fit comfortably and remain firmly in place despite high winds. It should have flaps to protect the ears. The twa-snouter, or deer stalker, has a lot to recommend it, as has the fur-lined North American shooting hat with long peaks and side flaps, even if less often seen, or favoured, in Britain. The colour of the headgear should merge with most backgrounds and an olive green or camouflage pattern is probably as good as any. Ideally the hat should be waterproof.

Shooting Jacket

There are many varieties of shooting jacket. It should be comfortable, roomy, allowing free swing and preferably with a lining and inner poacher pockets. Some of the modern materials are very hard to beat, being light, waterproof, tough and neither shiny nor noisy. Many of the shooting jackets offered for sale may be waterproof and comfortable enough but they are extremely noisy when moving through bushes and crawling through undergrowth on a stalk. It should be borne in mind that what may be suitable for roughshooting may not be suitable for stalking. It is also essential to have material that breathes, or is well ventilated, otherwise the roughshooter may end up dry on the outside and soaked with condensation inside. There should also be drainholes in the pockets, or the roughshooter may sometimes end up with a pocket full of water requiring to be emptied.

Inevitably the roughshooter will end up with more than one jacket for shooting and there are occasions when one will be more suitable than another. When stalking in woodland a good tweed merging with the background, or even a camouflage jacket, may prove ideal where a waterproofed cotton or nylon jacket would prove far too noisy. On the other hand, when walking out on the foreshore, or waiting for wildfowl to flight in wet and cold conditions, a thoroughly waterproof lined nylon or waxed cotton jacket may well be ideal, while a tweed jacket will merely become slowly sodden.

Leg Coverings

If trousers are worn they should be tough and comfortable. They should preferably be able to tuck into boots if required. Much the best wear for roughshooting really are knickerbockers or plus-twos, rather than plus-fours. Voluminous plus-fours tend to get very wet in damp roots or similar conditions and take a long time to dry out, leaving an unpleasant wet roll of cloth around the knees. Knick-erbockers or plus-twos do not get so easily wet around the knees and are also better for stalking on all-fours. Good thick shooting stockings worn under them should be held in place by a strap or velcro fastening. When conditions are wet, waterproof over-trousers, or better still side fastening over-trousers with pop studs or velcro fastening, are a quick and convenient way of staying dry. Also quite good are the waterproof boot tops which slip on and can be laced in position, conveniently keeping the lower leg dry.

The kilt is an excellent garment for the moor but sometimes not quite so good when stalking, or on low ground, unless the wearer is accustomed to it and knows how to cross barbed wire and similar obstacles without serious injury. It will dry out quicker than most garments and on the moor there is nothing to match it.

Binoculars

Many roughshooters will regard these as unnecessary and if you have twenty-twenty vision they may seem a little unnecessary. Even with such perfect vision, however, it is impossible to identify birds at half a mile or to say with certainty whether that patch of red is a fox or a roedeer lying snugly in a hollow or a patch of bracken. The lines of flight of pigeons on the shoot and where they are pausing to feed, the variety of duck just visible on the far side of the lake, the identity of that man seen just moving away down that old cart track:

these and many other things are identified by using binoculars. A small pair of tough pocket binoculars are essential for stalking and for a hundred other purposes on the roughshoot. They will prove an invaluable aid to the roughshooter, even if his eyesight is first class.

Telescopic Sights and Sight Aligner

It is worth buying the best telescopic sight that you can afford for the rifle. The type of graticule used is largely a question of individual preference, whether post and rails, or cross-hairs, or variants. A sight aligner as an aid to sighting-in the telescopic sights will soon pay for itself and is worth buying since the knowledge that the sights are correct is a great confidence booster.

The Dog

Next to the gun, the dog on the shoot is the roughshooter's foremost requirement. What breed of dog is chosen will inevitably depend to a large extent on the roughshooter's own preferences. The important thing is that the roughshooter's dog should be able to hunt the ground and find game for his master. In thick cover he must stay close at hand within shot, but on moorland it is desirable that the dog can quarter well out, in which case it is essential that he points and holds game rather than flushing it out of range. Although the pointer-retriever breeds are naturally capable in this respect there is no earthly reason why any dog cannot be trained on these lines. The spaniel will often prove a natural pointer, holding well to game, and a good labrador or retriever trained to hunt wide can also easily enough be encouraged to hold game even if the tail may not be consistently rigid, but moving gently. Such a dog can prove as efficient a game finder on a moor as most pointers and setters, or the pointer-retriever breeds. A good dog well trained, working in enthusiastic and happy understanding with its master is a pleasure to watch whatever its breed. The illusion that any one breed is better than another is one of the blinkered theories to be found in those who have bigoted minds and have not learned to appreciate good dog-work, or else just do not have sufficient experience and have themselves been taught by inexperienced and bigoted enthusiasts. There are many people who do not know what they are talking about in the dog world as in most others.

Any dog may prove an excellent gun dog for the roughshooter and I have seen mongrels and half-breeds which have proved surprisingly good, from half-bred Irish wolfhound lurchers to small Jack Russell crosses, down to three-legged springer spaniels of doubtful origin. But all have had the one great flaw that it has been impossible to breed from them with any likelihood of breeding true and getting a similar pup to follow them. In this respect it is always worth taking a pure-bred dog or bitch and training it to your requirements. When the time comes, as sadly it does eventually, when a replacement is required you may, if you have chosen a bitch, take a pup from her or, if a dog, take a pup of his breeding. In this way a sense of continuity is produced and it will be found that by such breeding many familiar traits will recur in the roughshooter's dogs over the years, enhancing the pleasure the owner naturally feels in his dog after a good performance.

REQUISITES ON THE SHOOT

Transport

The roughshooter will require some form of transport to take him to the shoot and preferably to take him and his companions, guns, dogs and equipment, around the shoot. This may often involve driving into and over fields, through miry, muddy gateways, along rough tracks and similar places, where four-wheel drive is a distinct advantage. The roughshooter's ideal transport is something capable of holding dogs, humans, guns and game comfortably and also of covering rough ground with ease. There are numerous such cross-country four-wheel drive vehicles on the market and something on these lines is a very sound investment. In common with most of my shooting partners and no doubt many other roughshooters, I have had many problems with vehicles bogged in ditches, stuck in muddy patches, bottomed out in deep ruts and just stuck in snowdrifts while shooting. These are amongst the common hazards of roughshooting but nowadays such problems can to a large extent be avoided if you can afford to buy a suitable four-wheel drive vehicle. In practice, on quite a few shoots it may pay a roughshooting partnership who have no suitable vehicle between them to invest in an old four-wheel drive landrover, for example, which is simply kept on the shoot to save their own cars becoming damaged or unnecessarily muddy and dirty.

Portable hide, camouflage netting, etc

It is always useful having a portable hide available. This may only consist of a suitable length of say ten yards of camouflage netting and four or so light steel poles on which to drape it. Numerous other forms of portable hide have been advocated by keen roughshooters over the years, from dyed net curtains on bamboo poles, to plastic pig netting suitably draped with strips of different coloured tights and most of them are perfectly adequate. Something light and portable which can be quickly erected whenever required saves the time involved in building a hide on the shoot, either for flighting duck or pigeon shooting.

Decoys

For shooting both pigeons and wildfowl on the roughshoot, decoys are an important asset. These can be of many varieties from the old solid wooden types which are now collectors' items to modern plastic, moulded polymer, or rubber inflatable decoys. The flat silhouette type of decoy may be preferred since more of these can be carried with comparative ease and, within reason, the greater the number of decoys laid out the better, although it is always important that they be set out in a lifelike and inviting natural manner.

Aluminium Extending Ladder

Along with suitable poles for lofting pigeon decoys, an aluminium extending ladder is a surprising asset on a roughshoot. By using it, lofted decoys can be set in many places that could never otherwise be reached. Sites may be found for treetop-level hides which may then be constructed comparatively simply, and with the ladder access is readily available. For stalking also they can provide access to good observation points for deer. High seats can be set up in a matter of minutes and foliage which is obstructing a view can be quickly and efficiently removed.

Cage Traps

Cage traps for mink, feral cats and foxes may be useful. Carting them to within easy range of the place where they are to be sited will often require a four-wheel drive vehicle, but they are an effective trap when suitably baited.

Traps and Snares

There are several varieties of approved traps still probably to be found around the countryside, but today the Fenn type traps are the only ones being manufactured for catching small ground predators, from weasels to mink. Placed in tunnel traps around the shoot these should prove very effective. How many are required depends entirely on the size of the shoot and the amount of time the roughshooter has available. Snares for foxes are also a very effective means of control, but experience and care are required when using them. Again, the numbers required must depend on the size of the shoot and the time available.

Pens, Feeders, etc

Depending on whether birds are to be reared and released, the roughshooter may require an appropriate number of rearing and release pens built on the shoot or carted into position. In any event, some feeders placed in strategic positions are almost inevitably required. These can easily enough be made from empty five-gallon oil drums.

Game Larder

At the end of any successful day the roughshooter will find that he needs a suitably fly-proofed larder in which to hang his game. This can be very easily made from an old cupboard with the doors and side panels removed, leaving only the framework. If nylon net material is then glued round the outside, a suitable wide opening door can be made by gluing velcro material in place, and a large roomy fly-proof larder is available. By insetting poles across the framework a considerable quantity of game can be hung so that air circulates freely but flies are kept out.

3

Grouse and the Moorland Roughshoot

THE RED GROUSE: *Lagopus Lagopus Scoticus*

The roughshooter who is fortunate enough to have a moorland roughshoot should enjoy superlative sport since grouse and the numerous other game likely to be found on most moors or their edges can provide enormous variety and interest. First and foremost there is the red grouse, *Lagopus Lagopus Scoticus,* which it is now generally agreed is a variant, peculiar to Britain, of the Willow grouse, *Lagopus lagopus,* found widely in Scandinavia. This dull scientific conclusion does not alter the proud boast that the red grouse, as such, is to be found and shot nowhere else but in these islands. It is common throughout the greater part of Scotland and southwards as far as Yorkshire, where there are some notable moors.

The birds with their reddish-brown plumage and noticeably feathered legs are about 15 inches from beak to tail and weigh up to 2 lbs. Their colouring and weight, however, can vary widely from area to area depending to a large extent on the feed available. Their call which is frequently heard on the moor sounds strangely like someone with a hoarse voice shouting 'Go-back. Go-back'. They usually begin to pair in November or December, nesting by April and incubating a clutch of from around six to as many as fourteen or more eggs, depending largely on the state of the feeding and the weather conditions.

Their principal feed is the young heather shoots, as well as most berries, especially blaeberries and cranberries in season, but they will also eat insects and corn when available. They have numerous disease problems, particularly parasitic worms, *Trichostrongylus pergracilis*, which build up rapidly and usually prove fatal when grouse are in poor condition following severe weather conditions. Another fatal disease, coccidiosis, is a parasite causing high mortality in the chicks. Worst of all in some areas is the effect of the sheep tick, which is very prevalent in parts of the highlands. So many may attach themselves to the young grouse that it dies from loss of blood and tick borne diseases. Numerous factors such as severe weather, frosted heather, lack of sufficient grit, which grouse require to aid their digestion, and uncontrolled predators, can very adversely affect grouse numbers. The uncontrolled growth of forestry with the inevitable increase in predators such as foxes is a considerable factor in the decline of grouse population in some areas.

THE BLACKGAME: *Tetrao tetrix*

Very often found in conjunction with red grouse are blackgame, or black grouse, *Tetrao tetrix*. The male is a large black bird with a prominent white patch on his rump and a very noticeably lyre-shaped tail. The female is smaller and closely resembles a grouse save for a white wing bar. These may still be found on the edges of moorland as far south as Devon, but mainly from the Borders northwards. The male is around 21 inches from beak to tail and the female around 16 inches. The weight of the male is around 4 lbs and the female around 3 lbs. They have a musical gurgling call when mating, but are notable mainly for their silent flight. Unlike the red grouse they are polygamous and an outstanding feature is their 'lek' or courtship dance, when the cocks form a circle displaying their distinctive lyre-shaped tails in front of the watching females. They usually lay around six to ten eggs depending on feeding and condition. They are strong fliers and deceptively fast.

THE CAPERCAILZIE: *Tetrao urogallus*

Also found in some areas of Scotland in similar habitat to blackgame is the Capercailzie, *Tetrao urogallus,* another member of the grouse family. Although more generally accepted as a bird of the pine woods, it is very often found on the edges of moors and even on quite low ground. The cock is the largest gamebird in Britain, measuring about 34 inches from the powerful beak to the tail and weighing around 12 lbs. He has an olive-brown back with a prominent white patch where the wing joins the body and a notably green-black breast, but the very prominent, fierce-looking, curved beak and large scarlet eye wattle make this bird quite unmistakeable when full grown. The hen though resembling a greyhen, or grouse in colouring is much larger and the square tail is a noticeable feature.

When young the cocks may at first sight resemble large pheasants but again the square tail is an obvious feature. Like blackgame they are notable for their silent flight, but during mating the call of the cock is unmistakeable, being exactly like the sound of a cork being pulled. Like blackgame they are polygamous and their mating to some degree resembles that of blackgame with a cock courting a group of attendant hens. The number of eggs laid may vary from five to ten and these are usually laid in a scrape in the undergrowth at the edge of the forest.

One of their principal foods is the buds and young shoots of conifers, but like blackgame they will eat almost anything from corn to blaeberries and insects. The interesting thing is that they were said to be extinct in the early 19th century and were re-introduced to Perthshire by Lord Breadalbane and Sir Thomas Fowell Buxton, a noted naturalist of the period, in 1837. The breeding stock they introduced has since spread throughout a large part of the Highlands north beyond Inverness and as far as Aberdeenshire in the east and Dumfriesshire in the south.

THE PTARMIGAN: *Lagopus Mutus*

One other bird of the grouse family which is less likely to be encountered by the ordinary roughshooter is the ptarmigan, *Lagopus mutus*, normally found only above the 2,000 foot level. With feathered legs like all the grouse family it is liable to considerable colour changes, turning pure white in winter and in summer subject to local variations. Normally the male is white-winged with a white chest patch, grey body and scarlet eye wattle. The female is greyer with buff markings. They are generally smaller than grouse, being about 14 inches from beak to tail and weighing under 2 lbs.

Although they generally pair in November or December they do not nest until June and the nest is usually just a scrape in the rocks with from five to nine eggs. They live on lichens, mosses, birch leaves and also blaeberries, cranberries and insects when available. Like the red grouse they also require large quantities of grit. They are seldom found below the Highland Line, being primarily a bird of the mountainside, although found on low ground in the Hebrides. They usually merge remarkably well into their stony background and remain squatting closely among the rocks they resemble until the last moment.

THE WOODCOCK: *Scolopax rusticola*

The woodcock, *Scolopax rusticola,* is more generally accepted as a bird of the woods, but is also commonly encountered on grouse moors, especially near the coast during migration periods from October through November. About $13\frac{1}{2}$ inches from tip to tail and weighing about 8–14 ozs, they have a grey or rufous browny plumage matching a dead leaf background. The sexes are indistinguishable to the eye, but their dumpy shape with rounded wings and long bill with very prominent eyes set in a rounded head are unmistakable. They mate early and lay over thirty-four eggs in a scrape in the ground from March to April. The males have a distinctive mating flight over a set route each evening, known as a 'roding' flight, during which they give a soft distinctive croaking call. They feed on worms, larvae and insects as well as seeds, dibbling with their bill in boggy ground.

Although there is a widespread resident population there are also regular migratory flights which arrive from the continent starting in October through to December each year. They can fly high and strongly as might be expected of migrant birds. Their flight in woodland is often erratic as they flit between the trees. This, combined with their comparative rarity, gives a sound basis to the old chestnut of the gamekeeper who ascribed his longevity to always falling flat whenever he heard the cry of 'Cock over'. It is easy for even an experienced shot to become excited and take a dangerous snap shot in such circumstances. Always take extra care when shooting woodcock amongst trees.

On the open moor they can often be quite a simple shot, but, wherever shot, they remain excellent eating. They should be roasted with the entrails, or trail, left in place. If this is allowed to soak into a piece of toast it is superlative eating, but it requires an experienced cook to produce it properly. Breaking the legs and drawing the sinews immediately after shooting as is often recommended strikes me as unnecessary since the woodcock thigh is anyway a minuscule mouthful.

THE COMMON SNIPE: *Gallinago gallinago*

The Common Snipe, *Gallinago gallinago,* is about $10\frac{1}{2}$ inches from the bill to the tip of the tail and weighs around 6 ozs. When flushed it makes a sound rather like tearing cloth often described as a dry 'Scaap'. The male makes a drumming, or bleating, sound with its tail feathers during mating display flights in the spring. The nest is a hollow usually in bracken, long grass or rushes and lined with grass. The clutch normally consists of four eggs and incubation takes place in March to April. They frequently lay a second clutch later in the season. They are readily distinguished from the very rare Great Snipe, which is the size of a woodcock, and the much smaller Jack Snipe, both of which are protected.

They will often run considerable distances when being dogged and even an experienced dog may have difficulty in holding them. When flushed they have an erratic zig-zag flight, rising rapidly. If flushed into the wind they will frequently gain height and turn back over the guns providing a very high sporting shot. Wisps of common snipe are likely to be found each year at the same time in the same feeding grounds, but to some extent their movements are dictated by the weather. High winds and freezing weather conditions will cause them to move their ground, although as with woodcock they are likely to be found in the same areas each year at much the same time. They are always likely to provide interesting and sporting shooting. Two on toast make a very good start to a meal.

Moor Management

As far as red grouse numbers are concerned the management of the moor is one of the most important factors influencing this. Correct heather burning, with small chequer-board patterns of burnt heather interspersed amongst older growth is the secret of plenty of grouse since this allows the birds to nest in the cover of the longer heather. They can retreat there when predators appear and at the same time find plenty of feeding in the young growth of small heather shoots in the freshly burned patches. It also provides chances of finding grit and blaeberries and other berry growth.

Burning in such a way on a moor of any size is no easy task and requires considerable experience and constant attention whenever the weather is remotely suitable. Too high a wind and the fire may get out of control, burning great swathes of heather and ruining the prospects for a few years. Insufficient burning when the time is right may be the result of long wet spells when it is impossible to get the heather burned and too much old growth may have to be left. The heather burning season is a short one between the end of the shooting season in December, and mid-March. By then the grouse are paired and contemplating nesting. Thereafter burning is rightly illegal.

Ensuring good supplies of grit on the moor where this is in short supply can be a very strong factor in ensuring good stocks of grouse. Water supplies on a dry moor are also a point to bear in mind. Otherwise the most that can probably be done is to ensure that predators are kept to a minimum and the birds allowed peace in which to breed.

Surprisingly, however, one of the important factors on a moor is to ensure that it is shot sufficiently. It is essential that the old birds, especially, are killed off before the end of each season. Grouse are unlikely to live more than two years in any event. Removing the old birds ensures a sufficient stock of young birds on the ground, but leaving too many may cause disease through overcrowding or insufficient feeding.

Dogging the Moor

If the roughshooter is using dogs on the moor, rather than driving, he will be in a position to know that each shot fired has either killed or missed a bird. No pricked or wounded birds will be left to spread disease, or fail to breed, as can easily happen on a driven moor. He will be able to kill off the old birds of the coveys as soon as the young birds are strong enough to look after themselves. By splitting up the coveys in this way he will ensure much more shooting throughout the season.

It has been my experience that where the birds are not driven but only shot over dogs they do not pack in large coveys as is seen on driven moors. This is in fact not natural behaviour but is probably induced by the fact that the birds are being regularly disturbed by driving and the formal grouping of the coveys has been broken up so that the young birds associate in groups with birds of the same sex, hence forming large packs of males and females. The same phenomenon may be seen amongst partridges where they are regularly driven by teams of beaters over the guns. This does not occur where the birds are regularly shot over dogs. The only groupings to be seen then are where a covey has not had the old birds shot and has remained as a self-contained unit, regularly flying away at the first sign of disturbance and generally a loss to the shoot.

Varieties of Game on the Moor

The majority of moorland roughshooting will only have grouse, and at the most blackgame, on it. Anything else, such as the occasional capercailzie on the edges, or a few coveys of partridges or even some pheasants on the lower ground near the fringes of the moor, is all a bonus. Many moors, however, will also have boggy patches where woodcock and snipe and even wildfowl may be encountered. There will also on many moors be quantities of blue hares to be found and again near the edges on the lower ground brown hares may also be encountered. In addition, of course, the ubiquitous rabbit and even pigeons may be found in places on many moors.

It is, naturally enough, only in very rare areas that grouse, blackgame and capercailzie, or grouse, blackgame and ptarmigan may all be shot on the same ground. I have only shot in two areas where this was the case, both in Aberdeenshire. The fact that ptarmigan are generally at a much higher level than either grouse or blackgame means that such ground must generally be part of a deer forest in the Highlands where disturbance with a shotgun and dogs is not desired during the stalking season.

The Deer Stalker's Viewpoint

Shooting grouse and stalking are often considered incompatible. This is the view of dedicated stalkers who do not wish to lose any deer from their ground and whose attitude to grouse and blackgame, or for that matter ptarmigan, is frequently jaundiced. Many old stalkers hold the view that grouse are nothing but a nuisance on good stalking ground since by rising cackling in the middle of a stalk they can sometimes be the cause of losing a good beast at the last moment. On hearing the grouse rising in alarm the deer will be alerted to danger and a shot may be lost. The same thing may be caused by an old ewe on the hill giving the alarm and alerting the deer in the middle of a stalk. There should be room for both grouse and deer on the same ground.

Individuality

Each moor has the great virtue of individuality. On one moor it may be that the roughshooter is looking down on the tops of chimney stacks and industrial development beneath him. On another nothing but a waving purple sea of heather is to be seen. On yet another, views over sea and cliffs may be commonplace. In any moor the ground is likely to have unexpected folds and even steep clefts which are not immediately visible to the eye. It is only after one or two seasons that the roughshooter is likely to have learned the minute geography of his moor. Even a comparatively small moor of a couple of thousand acres will take a lot of dedicated walking before the roughshooter can feel he knows where to expect to find birds, where he can expect them to fly and how to keep them on his own ground.

An Ideal Moor

For the past twenty years I have been fortunate in being the tenant of a small moor of two thousand acres which makes an almost ideal roughshoot. It has both grouse and blackgame, also both pheasants and partridges on the fringes. There are in addition considerable numbers of snipe and woodcock as well as wildfowl and all types of groundgame, with numerous rabbits, some brown hares and a few blue hares.

Five or six varieties may regularly be shot which is not so very exceptional, but the ground itself is, in my view, ideally varied. There are burns bisecting deep ravines and a stream meanders along one boundary, separating the moor from an ugly stretch of conifers. There are upland boggy patches, where duck and snipe are to be found, and stretches on the edges near the burn where rabbits abound, providing exciting shooting as they race towards their burrows on the steep hillsides.

Patches of bracken and gorse grow near the fringes where partridges and pheasants as well as occasional woodcock may be seen. There is also the likelihood of encountering blackgame around the edges of the forestry, while roe deer similarly may be seen in the evening and at dawn venturing onto the moor. There are not many such excellent moorland roughshoots to be found and after walking over it for the best part of a day many people have confessed that they found one day on it quite enough. That, of course, is part of the pleasure of a good moorland roughshoot. It is necessary to be fit when there are steep-sided glens with long heather to negotiate at an angle of over forty-five degrees in a blazing sun. Sadly a number of equally good neighbouring moors are now being steadily afforested and are disappearing under dull regiments of conifers, which can be nothing more than havens for foxes and crows.

Varied Rents

On ground where driving the birds is difficult roughshooting need not be expensive even today, despite the media image of grouse moors. I know one man, with a sweetshop in the Borders, who leases at a modest rent a small moor on which he shoots blackgame, grouse, snipe, pheasants, mallard and groundgame. With a stream running through it and one or two shelter belts of trees it is an ideal moorland roughshoot. Another acquaintance, a sporting postman, who keeps three gundogs in his second-floor council house flat, leases an interesting mainly low ground shoot with grouse on the edges, along with partridges, snipe, pheasants and groundgame. Such shoots are still to be found in Scotland and the north of England, but naturally it helps to live on the spot.

It is unlikely to happen again, but I once obtained the lease of a very good moor in Aberdeenshire for the rent of a brace of grouse whenever I shot it. It was on this moor that the dogs pointed young capercailzie close to the trees on the upper boundaries, and blackgame interspersed with partridges rose from the cornfields on the lower fringes. The grouse themselves were few and far between, principally because the heather was amongst the longest and coarsest in places that I ever remember. The moor itself was a very large bowl in the hills, very dry but with good light woodland above and cultivated fields below, in the flat of the bowl as it were. The capercailzie and blackgame clearly lived on the higher ground and moved down to the cornfields for feeding. They were thus to be found in between and provided enormous sport.

Comparative Flight Speeds

The first time grouse are seen in flight with blackgame it will be a surprise to see how very much faster the larger, bulkier, and at first sight clumsier birds are flying. A blackcock will leave a grouse behind with deceptive ease and in order to catch them in full flight it is necessary to swing fast. The same is also true of capercailzie and it was on this particular moor that I first saw these three birds all in flight at the same time with the capercailzie undoubtedly the fastest, even if by far the largest.

The capercailzie when encountered in woodland have the same knack as the woodpigeon of slipping out of the tree on the side opposite to the approaching gun. Like the woodpigeon, they will also sometimes make quite a noise with crackling of twigs as they take flight, although the flight itself is remarkably silent. If they are not seen in flight there will be no warning of their approach when driven through a wood. A successful shot, however, will be followed by a crashing of the branches and a heavy thump as the bird descends to earth.

Although, as indicated, ptarmigan are hardly likely to be encountered on a moorland roughshoot, both capercailzie and blackgame are very much a part of the moorland roughshooting scene. In Dumfriesshire and Ayrshire, but mainly in a broad moorland belt from Perthshire through Angus to Aberdeenshire and on to Moray, it is possible on a moorland roughshoot to encounter blackgame and capercailzie as well as grouse. The combination is certainly a very satisfying one.

Four-Wheel Drive

The moorland roughshooter will very probably have a larger stretch of ground to manage than the low ground roughshooter, but generally with comparatively larger stretches of unproductive ground. Even more than the low ground roughshooter he will probably find a four-wheel drive vehicle useful. If the moor is intersected by roads this may not be so necessary, but in other respects this may not be so satisfactory since easy access for picnickers, or town dwellers innocently exercising their dogs, far more than the occasional loss of birds hit by cars, or incidental poaching, is likely to make life difficult for the owner or tenant of such ground.

Trespass and Damage

It is hard to explain to the town dweller with a pack of noisy children and dogs that by picnicking on what to them seems like a sunny stretch of moorland in May, deserted by all but a few sheep they may be doing any damage. Yet by allowing those labrador-collie crosses or busy little terriers to roam around the ground freely while their children play ball amongst the heather they may be causing grouse to desert their nests, or their dogs may be eating the eggs or young chicks. It is easy enough with a group of hikers crossing apparently barren moorland for a grouse nest to be trodden on or even a hen bird to be crushed underfoot. Disturbance during the breeding season is the last thing any moorland tenant or owner will desire even if it is difficult to explain to the town dweller who does not understand the life of the wild.

On the whole, however, if properly approached most town dwellers are prepared to be reasonable when it is pointed out to them that they may be damaging the unseen wildlife around them. It is probably the wildlife predators themselves which are likely to prove most difficult to control. Foxes, mink, hawks, crows and other predators may inflict a great deal of damage on the moorland roughshoot, killing old and young grouse, pouncing on the sitting hen or stealing the eggs.

Traces of Predators

Only by covering the ground and examining each piece of evidence as it is found can the culprits be identified; the wings torn off the body and left behind by the fox raiding the hen on her nest; the tell-tale ring of feathers left by the peregrine as it stooped on the covey and killed off a young bird; the star-shaped trademark of the mink's feet as it crossed a muddy patch of ground; the fox droppings and the run alongside the fence with the traces of fur where the vixen comes onto the ground each evening; the all too numerous signs of eggshells with one end cracked open and sucked dry by the carrion crow; signs of the feral cat with the kill eaten and just the feathers remaining, though not in the neat circle left by the hawk; all these and more are likely to be encountered from time to time.

Poachers

A mere tuft of feathers found on the ground is usually a sign that a two-legged fox, or poacher, has been at work and a bird has been shot and picked by a dog. It is always worth keeping an eye open for stray cartridges or signs of such kills which show that poachers have been at work. On an unkeepered moor it is often difficult to prevent poaching but such poachers are seldom as much of a menace on moorland as the natural predators.

There are of course sometimes gangs of brazen poachers who quite systematically walk over a piece of ground in line with dogs and guns intent on having a good shooting day at the expense of the tenant or landowner. When approached they will usually say they have been given permission and name one of the neighbouring landowners. When it is pointed out they are off their own ground they will apologise profusely and depart. It is only when the neighbour is rung up that the deception is discovered, by which time it is probably too late.

On the moor I leased for a brace of grouse at the end of each shooting day the owner, an eccentric old sportsman, but not a man to miss a trick, saw such a bunch of organised poachers shooting his ground. He first rang his neighbour to check there was no mistake and then waited patiently by their cars for them to return. On their arrival he informed them they had been poaching. They gave the expected excuse that his neighbour had given them permission, but he was not having that and told them to hand over their entire bag of twenty brace or face the police. After a little blustering they handed over the grouse and went on their way.

'I let them have a brace for their pains,' he added, when telling the story.

Unfortunately poachers of this kind can have good sport at the expense of the tenant or owner, who may be reserving the moor for himself or his friends and finds it has already been shot. This is one of the hazards of renting a moorland roughshoot, but with the active assistance of the farmer it is less likely to arise. The presence of someone on the ground is always likely to prevent such brazen poaching and the single man with a dog is less likely to do much damage, although he too can be a tiresome nuisance.

Flight Lines

The knowledge of where the birds are likely to fly on the moorland roughshoot can be of great value. It is best, of course, to try to work the moor into the prevailing wind to make matters easier for the dogs. Grouse may be scented by dogs with good noses at as much as three hundred yards or even more. It is also astonishing how fast grouse can move even in thick heather and also how tight they will sometimes stay, even allowing themselves to be almost trodden on before rising and taking to flight. The moorland roughshooter who merely walks up his game with dogs working close at hand in front of a few of the guns will never find as many birds as the man who has wide-ranging pointers or setters, or pointer-retrievers. It is only once the moorland roughshooter has shot over such dogs that he will appreciate how much game he has been missing previously.

By knowing where the birds when flushed are likely to fly, usually along the contours of the slopes, it is sometimes possible to use the ground and place a gun or two in position in advance and thus arrange an impromptu drive. Since distances are likely to be much greater than on a low ground shoot this is not as easy an arrangement as it may be there. Generally the best that can be done where three or four guns are walking out on the moor is for two of them to take one side of a hill and two the other with the arrangement that one pair will halt at some previously arranged point where it is felt they may have a chance of waiting unseen by any grouse coming over them. By this means either pair of guns may flush birds which fly over the others and may sometimes provide very good driven shooting.

Driven Grouse

Occasionally when birds are very wary after a spell of wild and windy weather, especially late in the season, the only chance of getting near them may be to drive them. Alternatively, when there are numbers of wild old birds it has been found impossible to get near, or when blackgame are running fast in front of the dogs, the only solution may be to drive them, even with small numbers of guns. The general principle of driving is to start by driving the birds downwind. Once the birds have been moved downwind away from home it is a question of circumventing them and driving them back towards their home ground upwind. This is easier with dogs and, if there are convenient places to station the guns where they cannot be seen, may result in sport for both drivers with dogs and those waiting for the birds. It should be remembered that when guns and dogs are visible from one hill to another there is little point in going from the first hill onto the second. The grouse will have moved away into the dead ground on the other side of the further hill and this is the ground which should then be shot, either walking up with the dogs or driving from one set of guns to the others.

Over Dogs

Shooting grouse over dogs, however, can often be quite a testing process. Shooting either driven grouse or over the dogs early in the season is a very different matter to shooting the same grouse in late September or in October and November. Only if the old birds have been systematically shot and no birds have been browned is there likely to be any chance of getting near to grouse in October and November. Then the speed with which they rise and streak away, curling downwind, can be a revelation to those who have only dogged them in August and September. This is sporting shooting indeed.

Not only the grouse on the moor can move fast in front of a pointing dog, or provide challenging shooting. It is amazing how snipe can run and it often requires a good dog to point a snipe firmly after a twisting run of a hundred yards or more. Then if the gun can shoot it accurately in any sort of wind he is doing well and has every right to feel pleased with himself. Let no one decry that sort of shooting. It is not only a test of marksmanship, but also of fitness.

Blackgame Shooting

The blackgame in August and early September are usually easily enough dogged and shot. They will then at times sit very tight. The old birds will not have fully recovered from the moult and the youngsters will not have gained their full powers of flight. In late September and October it is another matter altogether. Then they will run or take flight at the first sign of danger. It may be necessary to station guns out of sight on their usual flight lines and attempt to dog them so that they take flight in the required direction. By following them up fast, at a full run, it is sometimes possible to get within shot, but once they have taken flight they are not likely to be easily found again that day and they will present a very challenging shot if driven over the waiting guns. A heavier shot such as four or five is also probably desirable for well grown blackgame or capercailzie, since they are strong birds and fast fliers.

The Shooting Season

It should be borne in mind that grouse come into season on 12th August and shooting ends on 10th December, while blackgame come into season on 20th August and their season ends with the grouse. Snipe come into season on 12th August and end on 31st January. Woodcock are different in England and Scotland, coming into season in Scotland on 1st September and in England on 1st October but in both cases the season closes on 31st January. Capercailzie are not in season until 1st October and their season ends on 31st January. It is thus only during October and November that all three species of grouse may be shot together in the few locations where this is possible.

Whether to shoot greyhens or not is always a question raised when blackgame are available. They are sometimes shot by accident before 20th August, a simple enough mistake to make on occasions but anyone so doing is usually subjected to a fine by his fellow guns varying from fifty pence to a bottle of whisky. When shooting capercailzie it is on the whole preferable to make hens sacrosanct even where they are comparatively common. Capercailzie are always said to taste of turpentine, but this is probably merely the result of the crop not having been thoroughly emptied as soon as the bird has been shot. All those I have eaten have been perfectly good eating after following this simple precaution, but the roughshooter fortunate enough to have these birds on his ground will wish to preserve them as much as possible. To a certain extent the same holds good with blackgame and here again a limit should perhaps be set on the number of hens shot. The chances are not likely to be very numerous in any event. The roughshooter fortunate enough to have blackgame on his shoot must make up his own mind and state the rules firmly beforehand.

Recording, Ageing and Sexing Grouse Shot

As well as recording the numbers of grouse shot at the end of the day it is desirable also to check and note the numbers of the different sexes and also the numbers of old and young birds shot. Young

grouse, like young partridges, can generally be readily identified by
their two outer primary wing feathers. In young birds these are
clearly pointed, but in older birds are rounded. The most accurate
way to test the age of grouse, partridge or pheasant of either sex,
however, is the bursa test. Young birds have a small blind hole on
the dorsal side of the vent. A feather or a matchstick can be thrust
about $\frac{1}{4}$ inch (6 mm) up this hole. Old birds have no bursa.

Sexing grouse can be very tricky at times and it is easy to make
mistakes. The chestnut red feathers are usually more distinct on the
chin, throat and breast of the cock birds. The hens are more liable
to be barred, or have lighter colouring. The red of the wattle may
be more pronounced on the cocks, but this is not a sure guide. A
regular record as accurate as possible of both the sexes and ages of
the birds shot is, however, naturally desirable.

Conservation

Any time expended on the moorland roughshoot, in observing the
wildlife and preserving it, is time well spent. The merlins, those
most delightful of hawks, the curlews, the whimbrels and the smaller
birds – the wheatears, the stonechats and above all the larks –
all make up part of a magnificent bird life, which the moorland
roughshooter should do his best to encourage. The fox, the mink,
perhaps above all the crow, and other predators of eggs, do not
distinguish between the nests of the birds they find. To a great extent
the moorland roughshooter acting as a conservationist is fulfilling a
much needed task in these days when so much upland ground lacks
keepers or protection from the natural killers in the wild.

4

Partridges on the Roughshoot

THE GREY PARTRIDGE: *Perdix perdix*

Habits and Habitat

The Grey Partridge, *Perdix perdix*, is one of the two varieties of partridge which may be encountered in Britain. It is native to the U.K. and is found more or less throughout the country, mainly on grassland, or farm land, but also on moorland edges and downland. It is a grey-brown short-winged bird with a rufous head and short rufous tail about 12 inches from beak to tail. The cocks weigh around 13–14 ozs while the hens are around 12 ozs. There is a rufous horse-shoe found on the breast which is usually more prominent in the cock bird, while the hen is normally greyer about the head, although this is not always the case. Their call is usually heard prior to and after flight, both as a warning and as an assembly call. It consists of a penetrating almost hissing sound, best described verbally as 'chissick'. They may be shot from 1st September to 1st February, but few sportsmen would consider shooting them on any scale at the very start or towards the very end of the season.

Mating

The grey partridge is normally found in coveys of from anything between half a dozen to sixteen or even more, but pairs off for mating around December or January. If the weather is then extremely severe they may re-form coveys, or even packs, prior to finally pairing. The pairs are strikingly devoted to each other and make excellent parents. The cock is often very gallant in defence both of his mate and the young. I have seen one fending off repeated attacks from a sparrow hawk with absolute fearlessness and enormous courage. Many other observers have seen similar defences of the young against attacks from hawks and even stoats. They will even face up to a hunting dog or cat, puffing themselves out, fluffing up their feathers and charging forwards with wings outspread to their full and hissing defiance. I have seen a dog completely bewildered and forced to retreat in the face of such an unexpected attack. It is enough to inspire admiration in anyone to watch this normally inoffensive bird behave so bravely. Anyone who has seen this sort of thing must have a great admiration for *Perdix perdix*.

The Wing-Trailing Technique

The grey partridge hen is also extremely courageous and an excellent mother. Even the tiny chicks are very sporting little birds. They will follow their mother and huddle under her spread wings when it is raining or danger threatens. Anyone who has seen a hen partridge protecting her young in this way will have been amazed to see the pile of small bumble-bee-sized chicks left in a heap behind as she rolls off them neatly and scuttles away emitting shrill cries of alarm with the usual wing-trailing technique of any feathered hen in the wild leading dangerous predators away from her young. It is always fascinating to watch the stray cat or hunting dog or other would-be hunter led astray by this performance. Once it has been led far enough away the mother suddenly recovers the use of her wings and soars away leaving her attacker standing baffled with mouth agape behind her.

Jugging

During the night a pair of partridges will sit tight, 'jugging', lying head to tail, thus keeping an all-round observation for any danger approaching. With the covey the parent birds will sit in a tight circle all with their heads outwards keeping each other warm. This may be seen from the small rings of droppings left behind as evidence of the practice each morning. The covey sitting tight in this way will all rise together swinging round with a confused whirring of wings and taking their direction from the parent birds. It is easy for the novice gun to be confused by this performance.

Nesting

The grey partridge is very selective about choosing a nest site and will often try out several possible sites before finally deciding on one. The nest itself, however, is merely a scrape in the ground lined with grass and despite these preliminaries is often to be found in an absurdly exposed position, close to a busy road or near a path or house. The eggs in such cases are probably best removed and placed under a broody hen in the hope that the bird will then lay again somewhere safer. The number of eggs laid may vary from ten to as many as twenty and two birds have been known to lay in the same nest. As noted, they are very good mothers and the cock bird is an excellent guard and defender.

Feeding

Grey partridge will eat a wide range of food, from insects, slugs and worms, to greens, such as cabbage and clover, to seeds of grass and weeds as well as corn. They will also eat berries from blaeberries to rowan berries and even young heather shoots. A great deal depends on their habitat, but as may be gathered they are fairly omnivorous. Insects are, however, vital to their survival and this can be a limiting factor in a cold wet spring.

Diseases

Like the red grouse, grey partridge are subject to attacks of the parasitic infection coccidiosis, which causes death mainly amongst the chicks. The chicks also often die of pneumonia brought on by wet weather when they are unable to keep dry. Hence, along with lack of insect feeding, very wet weather in June, when they are hatching out, is likely to have disastrous effects on the wild partridge population. They are also subject to a minute parasitic worm, *Tricho-strongylus tenuis*, similar to the worm affecting grouse, only smaller, which passes through droppings and into plants and so returns to the partridge. Too great a concentration of birds on the ground is therefore, as with grouse, undesirable and can lead to disease from this source.

Flight

The grey partridge is a very sporting bird and, as noted, is found more or less everywhere in Britain except on mountain tops. Unlike the silent flight of the grouse, the coveys rise with a distinctive whirring of wings. As with grouse, however, the old birds tend to rise first and it is advisable to try to shoot them early in the season so as to split up the coveys and provide more sporting shooting. If the old birds are left they will in any event tend to drive the youngsters off the ground in the spring and this in itself may result in fewer birds.

FRENCH, OR RED-LEGGED PARTRIDGES:
Alectoris rufa

The French, or Red-Legged Partridge, *Alectoris rufa*, as the name implies is not a native bird although found now in many parts of Britain. It was introduced from France into Richmond Park in the 17th century by Charles II and has since steadily established itself. In the last decade or so, especially as it has been found that it can readily be established artificially and will provide useful shooting, it has become almost as widespread as the native bird. On my own shooting in Scotland I have never previously seen the red-legged partridge but in the past year or two it has appeared on both low ground and moorland, clear evidence that it is establishing itself over an ever wider area since to my knowledge it can only have been bred on one or two estates some miles away. It is, however, a welcome asset.

Habits and Habitat

As is indicated by its alternative name, the French partridge differs from the native greys in having red legs. In addition, it has a red beak and a grey crown and very obvious white eye stripes as well as a white throat patch. The cocks are distinguishable by a small spur knob on the leg, which may be felt on the young birds, even if not visible, but some old hens develop this too. They are larger than grey partridges, the cocks being about $13\frac{1}{2}$ inches from beak to tail and weighing 16–18 ozs, with the hens rather smaller. When seen together it is thus usually easy enough to sex them by size alone.

While at a distance they may be mistaken for the grey partridge, their flight and call are both different. They will not take flight so readily and will often run considerable distances, but when they do fly they do so boldly and usually a good deal further than the grey. Their cry is a rather harsh 'chuk-chuk', which is often heard when flushed.

General

Both the times of matings and the mating habits of the French partridge are similar to the grey partridge. A notable feature is that both cock and hen will incubate the eggs. Sometimes two clutches are even laid by one hen, the second being incubated by her mate, although there is a tendency for fewer eggs to be laid per nest. For years they have had the reputation of being quarrelsome birds and driving the greys off their nests, but this is now to some extent discounted. There is, however, the fact to be taken into account that they require a distinctly larger territory than the grey and thus there are likely to be fewer birds on the ground compared with the grey.

The advantage of the red-leg is probably that it is easier to rear artificially. They are also possibly hardier birds, able to survive in more difficult circumstances. Whether in fact they provide such good sport for the roughshooter is open to question. On the whole they seem to be sporting birds and the suggestion that they are not as good for the pot is probably largely a question of cooking. Like the grey partridge they are best reared artificially on ground where there are no other coveys established as otherwise they are liable to be driven off the ground by the wild birds already present.

Ageing Partridges

Ageing partridges, like ageing grouse, can be done very simply by examining the two outer primary wing feathers. In young birds these are quite distinctly pointed, but as the birds grow older with constant wear on landing and take-off (vide: signs of take-off and landing in snow) these feathers become rounded. The young red-legs also usually have a white tip to their outer primaries which disappears after the first season. The bursa test, as with grouse or pheasants, is also a sure test of age. Furthermore, the skull of a young bird is very soft, while that of an old bird is much harder.

Rearing Artificially

Unlike grouse it is not difficult to rear partridges artificially from the egg and release them on the shoot effectively. Grouse may be reared easily enough, but have not yet been released effectively in the wild. With artificial brooders and modern methods it is not difficult to rear young partridges from the egg and it is comparatively simple to release numbers in the wild. This is most likely to be successful on ground where there are no established coveys, otherwise the wild birds may drive them off their territory. Barren pairs on the other hand will generally take over a young covey very quickly.

Releasing

The main principle is to keep to covey-sized numbers when releasing the young birds. As noted, if the covey is released near an old barren pair they are generally taken charge of by the old birds in a very short space of time. If the ground has no other birds on it, however, they should be set out in good-sized strong vermin-proof pens. Some 12–20 birds may be put out together in a suitable area on the roughshoot where they are sheltered to some extent from winds and driving rain and where the covey has room to establish its 'territory'. First one bird is released and then a day or so later two more, and gradually in this way over a fortnight or three weeks the birds are released from the pen, returning to 'jug' near their still-penned companions at night. The same principle works perfectly well with birds which have been reared under a broody hen.

While this method is very dependent on keeping predators away from the pen during the release period, it can be very effective in areas short of birds. It can result in producing one or two more coveys of birds on the roughshoot and establishing a breeding stock for years to come. It is therefore well worth the effort if possible, even if the results are a failure at the first attempt. With experience, the roughshooter may well be able to increase his partridge stocks in this way.

Improving the Wild Stock

On most roughshoots with any reasonable stock of wild birds, it will probably be sufficient to keep down predators and try to note the position of each nesting pair and protect them as far as possible.

Above: Pheasant nest by roadside open to predation.

Below: Backyard rearing under broodies.

Above: Incubator rearing.

Below: A rearing pen used as a makeshift release pen and feeding point.

Above: Bird's eye view of gun without hat or facemask, (*below*) bird's eye view of gun with hat.

Top: Hanging the game on the outside of the Land-Rover.
Above: A line of beaters on a driven day.

Opposite: Climbing up to a treetop platform.

This page: Gun in position at tree-top level. Two different examples of tree-top platforms.

Opposite: Waiting for duck on the river bank.

A successful stalk on geese.

Shooting grouse on the moor.

Nests which are apparently too obvious may be protected by means of additional cover in the way of extra twigs or vegetation laid in place by way of camouflage. If it is desired to examine the nest it should be approached carefully using a light hazel wand to part the grass around it gently. Approaching nests too often is likely to be disastrous since predators such as foxes, stoats or weasels may follow the pathway or scent left by the roughshooter and may thus be led unwittingly to the nest by the would-be protector.

Whether the roughshooter rears some partridges, either red-legs or grey, on his shoot, or whether he simply does his best to protect and increase the wild stock already there, he will wish to obtain the best possible sport from them. As with grouse, a great deal of sport may be had from dogging partridges, while equally fine sport of a different nature may be had from driving them successfully. It should be possible for the roughshooter who has watched over his birds carefully and has learned their favourite flight lines to be able to drive partridges much more successfully than he is likely to be able to drive grouse. To begin with, since they fly shorter distances it is often possible to drive the same birds two or three times, whereas if successful in driving grouse twice the roughshooter is doing very well.

Catching up

The covey instinct can lead partridges readily enough into a trap. If one leads the way into a cage trap the others will follow blindly. This behavioural instinct was well-known and readily exploited by the trappers in the Middle Ages, who would drive partridges slowly towards a gap in which a net was concealed. Once the first was in the rest would follow and the net would then be closed and the entire covey caught.

On the whole it is not really desirable for the roughshooter to attempt to catch up any wild birds on his shoot. Grey partridges which have laid once will not lay a great many eggs in their second season. Red-legs are rather different and may even lay more eggs in their second season. Greys are much wilder in captivity and are liable to damage themselves seriously by leaping up sharply and hitting their heads against any solid top to a cage. For this reason it is highly desirable to have netting roofs to any cages for partridges, but even then the greys may damage themselves by leaping up wildly at the approach of any stranger. If the roughshooter is intent on rearing partridges it is probably best for him to stick to red-legs and to start with eggs bought from a game farm. It is only if he is an experienced game rearer and living on the ground that he is likely to be successful catching up and rearing from his own stock and in this case he will probably have sufficient birds on the ground already.

Winter Feeding

Feed for partridges, especially during spells of hard weather, when the snow is on the ground and natural feeding is scarce, becomes very important. Useful feeding patches can be established in sheltered patches in the lea of woods, or hedges, where grain can be set out, either in feed hoppers or in straw, giving the birds something to scratch. It is important to accustom the birds to the feeders by feeding well beforehand and also to keep feeding once the shooting season is over. This indeed is most important on any roughshoot. By feeding, the birds are kept concentrated on the shoot and do not stray off to neighbouring ground where they may settle down and breed for the coming year.

Partridge Population

It is, of course, impossible to lay down any hard and fast rules as to bird populations on any given acreage since so much must depend on the natural feeding available, the general habitat and shelter and so on. It used to be estimated that on good feeding ground a pair of grey partridges might be expected every five to eight acres or so, while red-legs are likely to require three or four times that area. Naturally enough in ordinary grassland without much in the way of feeding these figures would be greatly increased and red-legs would probably require something like sixty acres, while the grey might require something like thirty.

The Start of the Season

Shooting partridges should not normally start until October when the young birds are generally strong on the wing. Shooting 'cheepers' or young birds not fully grown, which fly weakly with a cheeping sound after the parent birds, is thoroughly unsporting as well as foolish since these are the birds which provide the most sport later in the season and some should in any event be spared for next season to breed. The same, of course, holds good with shooting similar young grouse on the moor in August. As indicated, in both cases it is desirable to shoot the old birds first, once the coveys are old enough to look after themselves. Slaughter of the innocents at any time is a thoroughly foolish and unsporting practice.

The only birds which should be shot in early September, unless it is an unusually forward year with all the birds strong on the wing, should be the old barren pairs. These are anyway unlikely to breed again and are better out of the way since they are likely to drive young healthy stock off their territories in the spring. In general no partridges should be shot while the corn is still standing. Not only are most birds likely to be in the cover of the cornfields, but any that are found in the open are sure to fly there immediately. It is, of course, thoroughly undesirable to follow up birds, or send dogs for wounded game, into standing corn which may thus be laid, or unnecessarily damaged.

Selective Shooting

The whirring sound as a covey of partridges rises can easily startle a novice and cause him to become over-excited. Since they often tend to rise in a fairly closely-packed group it is important to take aim either at the first to rise, or at the outside members of the covey and avoid 'browning' several birds, or firing into 'the brown', i.e. the mass of birds. This is likely to result in one or more birds being wounded. Two or more birds may fall, but they are seldom dead and it is a deplorable novice mistake. It is always imperative to select individual birds and to kill them cleanly from a covey, be they partridges or grouse. Killing more than one bird with a single shot is generally indicative that a clear aim has not been taken and is a matter to be deplored, not a matter for congratulation. The same is true, of course, of any shot at birds flying close together which kills more than one.

At the same time it should be noted that when an old pair rise together they will often fly close to each other within about thirty yards and it is sometimes possible quite deliberately to hold the shot so that both fall dead inside the spreading pattern of the shotgun at that range. This is not advocating trick shooting, nor is it suggested that this is necessarily desirable. It is merely that I have seen this done by an expert game shot more than once as a deliberate piece of shooting. It is not suggested that a novice should try this any more than intentionally browning a covey.

Learning the Range

Out of range shots should also always be avoided. It is important for the novice to get a clear idea of range as soon as possible and work out how far birds are from him when taking the shot. Measuring the distance to where a bird has fallen after being shot, by pacing it out, may start to give the beginner an idea of range. Calculating how far a tree or bush is away and then pacing it out will also help to accustom the novice to gauge distance effectively. Until he is sure of his ranges it is impossible for him to expect to shoot properly. Practice in this respect is all important.

Watching the Flight

Grey partridges especially will not normally fly more than four or five hundred yards and when they take flight the covey should be watched carefully, particularly if any shots have been fired. If the bird that has been fired at does not fall immediately, it is possible that it was in fact hit and may still fall some distance away. It may even land and run some distance before falling over stone-dead. It is generally worth following up any bird that has been seen to flinch to the shot and casting a dog onto the line where it was seen to pitch (see page 60). A bird with a leg down may fly quite a distance but will probably not rise again and should always be followed up until found. With both legs down it may still fly quite far, but is certainly going to die and is usually easily enough found where it lands, if the line has been noted correctly. These points, of course, apply equally to grouse and most other birds as well as partridges.

Partridge Reactions

It is important to realise that the instinct of partridges, like grouse, or for that matter most gamebirds, is either to squat, or head for the nearest cover, at the approach of danger. When danger is seen or heard approaching in the distance they will often scuttle away at considerable speed, their heads held low to conceal themselves. Normally their tendency when caught feeding in a field of stubble is to head for the nearest hedge. If flushed they also have a tendency to head for the nearest patch of cover, such as a nearby field of roots. Once in roots their tendency is again either to squat in concealment or to run down the drills away from danger. These natural reactions can sometimes be used effectively to the roughshooter's advantage. For instance, it should always be remembered that a winged bird down in a stubble field will head for the nearest hedge or cover, and the dog may be sent in that direction accordingly with a good chance of success.

When walking even the most seemingly bare grass field it is advisable always to walk into, or send a dog into, each corner as it is approached. The tendency is for the birds to run up the hedgerows and squat in the corners before taking flight. Many an innocent novice has been surprised by a covey rising almost at his feet as he has been in the act of swerving away on approaching the corner of a field. Being taken by surprise his two quickly snatched shots almost inevitably fail to register, but hopefully the lesson has been learned always to be ready for game towards the end of even a seemingly empty field. It is then, near the hedge, as the guns and dogs approach it that any game is most likely to be flushed. Only too often, with dogs running too far ahead and failing to point, the game is bumbled up out of shot the far side of the hedge. It is always worthwhile slowing up slightly as the hedge is approached in such circumstances and always being ready for a shot, especially in the corners of each field.

Sometimes it is possible to utilise knowledge of partridge flight lines, as with grouse, to obtain some excellent driven shooting, even in almost open downland. Like grouse, partridges prefer to follow the contours of the ground. As with grouse, it is desirable on open downland to start by driving the partridges downwind and away from home for the best results. Like grouse on the moor, they will often fly surprisingly high when curling round and, since there are no trees to measure them against, it is often difficult to gauge how high they are and when to shoot. The birds which do not follow the contours but turn sharply downhill, flying off the downland slopes and coming downhill over the guns, can be very hard to hit. They can also be most satisfactory when cleanly killed, falling a long way behind the line.

Driving Partridges

By walking up the stubbles first thing in the morning the coveys out enjoying the morning sunshine may be driven into the cover of a root field. With luck one or two birds may be shot in the process. Once all the stubble or grass fields surrounding the roots have been driven the roots themselves may be walked up. With one line of guns behind the hedgerow, preferably upwind, the other guns and beaters may walk across the drills into the wind and drive the birds across the hedge over the waiting guns.

The guns should be thirty yards or so back from the hedge and the higher it is the better their sport. They should try to shoot the moment the covey appears above the hedge. In this way the birds should swerve sideways across the guns on either side, providing challenging shooting. Needless to say neither the guns waiting behind the hedge, nor the guns in the field, should shoot forward when the beating line is approaching within range. Then, obviously, for safety's sake any birds shot should only be taken behind.

Use of Root Fields

As indicated above, one of the more successful ways of driving partridges is to walk them in from the stubble fields into roots or rape. The coveys can then be split up and shot successfully providing a great deal of sport with individual birds and small groups of twos and threes rising one after the other. It may well be possible to place three or four guns behind a hedge while two or three zigzag across the roots towards them. (N.B. It is essential always to walk across the drills, never down them or the partridges will simply run ahead down them and into the hedge.) It is usually desirable to make several beats in a large root field providing some good driven shooting as well as possibly some interesting birds in the root field itself. There can, however, be few more testing birds than a covey of driven partridges flying at speed over a high hedge and splitting abruptly at the sight of the waiting guns on the far side. A well taken right and left in front, neatly killed from the curving twisting covey is a test of skill indeed and when successful will not be easily forgotten.

Where possible the roughshooter should always try to arrange the cropping on his shoot so that there are two fields of roots within easy distance of each other. This is the ideal situation: it may then be possible to drive all the birds from the surrounding stubbles or grass fields into one field of roots and from there drive the majority into the second field of roots. The drive may then be reversed if there are sufficient birds and many of them may be driven back once again. Such a process, of course, should not be carried too far and after two successful drives the birds should be spared to rest and recover.

Very large root fields with too few guns and beaters can be somewhat daunting. The ideal is to get the farmer if possible to cut them into smaller individual sections by cutting a broad swathe down the middle. In this way they can often effectively be turned into two fields of roots and birds may be driven from one field into the other. They can thus provide much better sport for the roughshooter.

Sometimes in a very large root field with only a few roughshooters available the most effective method is to start at one end of the field, moving in a circle starting into the wind and steadily turn in decreasing circles into the centre of the field. With the dogs quartering the ground fairly closely in front of the guns this can prove a surprisingly successful method of shooting a very large field and by then reversing the process from the centre those birds which have been missed may well be flushed, providing the roughshooter with some excellent sport.

Over Dogs

Shooting partridges over dogs can also be very interesting sport. As with grouse on the moor, it is possible to shoot partridges in downland, or even lowland shoots over dogs. The same principles as with shooting grouse over dogs should be applied. Three or four guns following behind the dogs should close in when the dogs come on point. Normally they will do best to work into the wind, but sometimes it may prove more sensible to start off downwind and then turn upwind on the return beat. A great deal, as always, must depend on the ground and the prevailing wind and weather on the day.

Adapting to Conditions

With partridges and with grouse, or indeed any game, the roughshooter must always be prepared to adapt his proceedings to the weather and the wind, also to the time of year and the ground. It is improbable that partridges which have suffered a series of wet and windy November days are going to remain sitting tightly in the bare stubbles. To try to dog them then is simply asking for a blank day.

It is always necessary to put oneself in the place of the birds and consider what one would be doing in such circumstances. If there are no roots conveniently placed any other suitable cover is likely to prove attractive. For instance, a thin windbreak of trees with a little undercover might be used as an alternative shelter. If this is carefully approached the birds may well still provide sporting shots. It is by observing the birds' behaviour at all times and by thinking out where his birds are likely to be at each stage of the day and why, that the roughshooter should be able to obtain the maximum sport from his shoot.

If the weather conditions have been soaking wet and the root fields themselves are wet and cold it is unlikely even if the birds are driven into them that they will stay there long. If in such circumstances the roughshooter starts to drive the birds from the stubbles slavishly into the roots and expects them to remain there while he systematically drives the other stubbles as well he deserves to be disappointed. The birds are unlikely to stay in the wet any longer than they can help. It never does to stick routinely to any method of shooting when conditions are clearly against it.

It is important always to consider the weather and ground conditions and try to work out how they may have affected the birds. The advent of the first hard frosts for instance will usually make coveys of partridges, and for that matter grouse also, sit very tight, even if they have been quite wild in previous days. Then walking up with the dogs may be surprisingly effective when only a few days previously the same birds had been rising well out of shot at the roughshooter's approach.

If the roughshooter's first attempts to find birds are unsuccessful he would do well to stop and try to work out why they have failed. He should then change his tactics according to what he has observed. For instance, it may be that after a night of heavy rain the birds are all trying to get dry in the open and are taking flight at the first sign of approaching danger. It may then be necessary to send some guns round under cover to wait in the likely flight lines and use the minimum remaining guns to act as beaters. Simply continuing to shoot in the usual way without any hope of success is absurd. The roughshooter should always adapt to the circumstances he finds on the ground just as the wildlife itself is doing. It is only by thinking on these lines that he is likely to have good sport.

Limiting the Shooting

With both grouse and partridges, however, at no time should the roughshooter shoot more than the number of birds that is reasonable. Early on in the season he should work out how many birds he has on the shoot and calculate on that basis how many it is sensible to shoot if he is to leave a sound breeding stock for the coming year. Nor must he forget to make due allowance for the natural casualties in the wild that are bound to occur.

The roughshooter should never be greedy. It is very easy to say that one more shot will not matter. It is far better to let an easy shot go late in the season and forego an extra bird in the larder. There is every chance that such a bird spared towards the end of the season may mean as many as a dozen more birds the following season. It should be in watching the number of birds on his shoot thrive and increase that the roughshooter gains his greatest reward.

5

Pheasants on the Roughshoot

THE COMMON PHEASANT: *Phasianus colchicus*

The common pheasant, *Phasianus colchicus*, is, surprisingly enough, not a native of these islands, but was probably introduced by the Romans. It is now so common that it hardly merits description. The cock bird with its handsome dark-green head, frequently with a white collar around the throat and very variable plumage has a long tail, while the female is usually a grey-brown with a shorter tail. The cock is around 30–35 inches from beak to tail, weighing around 3 lbs and the hen is around 21–25 inches and around $2\frac{1}{2}$ lbs.

Their cry is a strident crow, sounding like 'Cock-up, cock-up', which may be heard frequently when about to roost, or in response to thunder, gunshot and similar loud noises, and when alarmed. The cock birds will often take flight with this call which a novice shot may find very disconcerting. In addition to the common pheasant there are numerous different varieties, particularly noteworthy perhaps being the melanistic mutant, in which both cock and hen are a very dark colour, with the soles of the feet a pale yellow.

Habits and Habitat

Pheasants are polygamous and generally mate in March or April. If too many cocks have been left over from the previous shooting season the hens may find themselves being harried unduly and will not get peace to nest. This is the reason for trying to reduce the number of cocks towards the end of the shooting season by holding 'cocks only' days. This is often achieved more effectively at the beginning of the season before they have learned to leg it at the sounds announcing the start of a shoot.

They are commonly found in woodlands, but they really like swampy, boggy ground and are generally to be found anywhere on agricultural land, in corn or root fields. In winter they may be found in hedgerows and stubble fields, or almost anywhere within range of suitable feeding. They are also sometimes encountered on the fringes of moorland, or on occasions even surprisingly far out on a moor. The hens will nest almost anywhere but it is usually just a simple scrape in the ground lined with grass. They may lay anything from eight to sixteen eggs and the incubation period is around twenty-three to twenty-seven days.

Diet and Diseases

Pheasants will eat almost anything and to a large extent their feeding reflects their surroundings. For instance, they will eat berries, grain, nuts, beech mast and insects, worms, leather-jackets, slugs, even field mice. It can thus be readily appreciated that reared in large numbers they may cause serious damage to growing crops and it is worth bearing in mind that the shooting tenant may be held legally responsible.

Like most gamebirds they are liable to catch the parasitic infection known as coccidiosis, which causes considerable mortality in chicks. The chicks may also catch pneumonia if they get very wet and this, combined with lack of insect life in a cold wet spring, as with partridges, can have a disastrous effect on them. In addition, they are liable to attack from the Gape worm, which infests the lungs and windpipes of chicks, particularly reared birds. Gapes, as it is generally called, is curable, but may cause considerable mortality.

Flight

The cocks are generally much better and more ready fliers than the hens, although a well-grown hen can also fly extremely well. The cocks have a tendency to fly straight upwards in woods until clear of the trees, giving their strident call at the same time, in a manner the novice shot is likely to find very startling. When it has gained height a pheasant will often set its wings and glide downwards for a considerable distance. Although it is not always apparent it can also be gaining speed while gliding with set wings, and with a cross wind it may also be drifting quite far sideways at the same time, which can make judgement of oncoming shots very difficult at times. It is the presentation of such challenging birds which can make driven pheasant shooting both interesting and worthwhile.

Pheasant Shooting

Almost more than any other form of shooting on the roughshoot pheasant shooting is what you make it. It can be the tamest of slaughter, bum-punching wretched wet birds at barely thigh-level in a field of soaking kale, or slaughtering birds barely shoulder-high driven out of a half-grown plantation. Alternatively it can be splendid sport with old cock birds, products of several generations of birds bred in the wild, hunted half-way up a steep hillside before launching themselves skywards into a high wind and curling back over the guns presenting the most challenging of shots. Such birds rocketing off a steep slope and almost out of range will stay in the mind for years and it is that sort of bird which makes a roughshooting day memorable.

Driven pheasant shooting properly organised may present many such birds, but may also vary greatly. To my eternal disgust I once watched a young man who was old enough to have known better slaughter over fifty half-grown, half-tame, reared pheasants streaming out low on one beat of a driven pheasant shoot on which I was adviser. He did not even kill a number of them cleanly, for my dogs picked several strong runners in the strip fifty yards behind him where I was standing.

He chose to ignore my shouted advice to leave them alone and I even heard him boasting subsequently that he must have accounted for half the bag that day. I was unable to resist telling him that while that might be true he should have been ashamed of himself. I am not sure even now that he fully understood what I meant, but it is that sort of mindless butchery which is enough to put anyone off shooting, barring the most thoughtless and mindless yobbo.

Rearing

Pheasants are easily enough reared from the egg to poult stage by using a small incubator. Almost any convenient shed may be used for this sort of back garden rearing of say a hundred or two hundred birds. Releasing them on the roughshoot so that they stay there is the main problem (and is a good reason why gamekeepers earn their name), quite apart from preventing them being taken prematurely by predators from foxes and mink to two-legged equivalents.

Releasing

It is virtually impossible to release any game on the shoot without someone living on the spot, or close at hand, being available to help and at least keep an eye on things. Without the known presence of someone in the vicinity a pen full of pheasants, or for that matter a coop full of partridges, is likely to prove too much of a temptation to some light-fingered rogue. While still unable to fly properly they are also prone to attack by predators and constant watchfulness is required.

If a release pen is impracticable on the roughshoot for one reason or another, it may be possible to rear a clutch or two of eggs under broody hens. Bantams are particularly good for the purpose. These may be reared in the back garden and when judged to be sufficiently well-grown they may be transported to the shoot. If then released in a suitable sheltered piece of woodland and regularly fed they may well survive and prove a useful addition to the roughshoot. If the hen survives she may be caught up before the shooting season begins and used again the following year.

The Release Pen

Siting the release pen is all-important and may often be extremely difficult. A sunny sheltered spot is desirable, but there should be water available and it must be easily accessible for feeding. On the other hand it should not be easily visible from a road, or too easily approached by poachers, who might remove all the birds. Ideally it should enclose a small copse or similar area, providing both shade and small bushes and trees to encourage the young birds to roost and provide protection from winds and rain. The undergrowth should not be too thick for young birds to penetrate. It is also important that it is not part of one of the main drives, where it will suffer frequent shooting close to it during the season or the birds will naturally desert it. It should never be shot and should be a place of sanctuary to which the birds feel it is safe to return after being driven elsewhere for shooting.

The pen should be wired in with wire netting, not stretched too tight and, of course, not nailed to any trees. It should be turned at top and bottom to deter predators and there should preferably be no sharp corners. Curved wire netting guides leading in to predator-proof entry pop-holes should be provided. The Game Conservancy provide a very good guide on the subject which is to be recommended to any would-be pheasant rearer on a roughshoot, who wishes to rear his own pheasants and build a release pen for them.

Electric Fence

A strip around the wire should be mowed with a grass cutter to give the poults ready access. An electric fence wire round this mown area will deter predators such as foxes and stray hunting dogs, or cats. Tunnel traps set round the release pen well-staked to prevent poults blundering into them and snares to catch foxes venturing too close are both desirable preventatives. The six weeks or so in which the poults are in the pens prior to learning to roost and fly sufficiently are always full of anxiety. It is virtually essential that the rough-shooter who rears pheasants on his shoot spares the time to be present every day during this period. It may, of course, be possible to share the duties between the members of the roughshoot and thus share the burden. In any event it will be an anxious period as every gamekeeper will testify.

Keeping the Poults from Straying

Once the poults are sufficiently grown, however, the problem remains of keeping them on the shoot. Regular feeding, morning and evening at the same time, with a similar whistle and regularly dogging the birds quietly back to the release pen is probably the only solution. Once again it is simply not feasible unless the rough-shooter lives close to the shoot and is prepared to spend the necessary time involved in what, although interesting, is undoubtedly an extremely burdensome chore.

Game Farm Surplus Hens

Most game farms offer for sale numbers of young hens which have been used for laying eggs. Such birds can be bought comparatively cheaply and may be released on the shoot instead of poults. The recovery ratio from such birds is, however, usually dismal. The reason for this is that on being released in a strange area they are likely to stray, since they have no reason to remain on the ground. If penned for a period and then released the ratio may be higher, but the point of buying these birds is generally because there is no release pen available. They may with luck lay a few eggs and rear a small brood if they can be kept on the ground; one way to ensure this is to make a temporary release pen of light nylon netting or use a rearing pen as a substitute. Since they are able to roost, this may hold them long enough to allow them to settle down and acclimatise to the area and accustom them to the feeding routine. The problem of predators, of course, with such a pen is much greater and trapping precautions need to be greatly increased.

Wild Birds

As with partridges, a good deal can be done to encourage wild birds to stay on the ground and breed successfully. Predator control and provision of good feeding throughout any hard spells of weather after the shooting season has finished will help to ensure that the wild stocks remain on the ground. Careful watch for nesting hens should locate a number of nests and these should be protected as far as possible. Tunnel traps and fox snares in the likely approaches for ground predators may be a wise precaution and, where necessary, the addition of some twigs or leafy cover to protect them from the eyes of egg-thieving crows or magpies. As with partridge nests, however, it is advisable to have a care about examining them too closely or too frequently as this may well prove counter-productive by actually leading possible predators to them.

Establishing a Routine

When it comes to shooting pheasants the important thing is not to drive them off the ground, since pheasants anyway have a ready inclination to stray and the hens especially may wander a matter of a mile or more simply in search of feed, if plentiful supplies are not made available. It is important to establish early on the likely places that pheasants will most favour on the ground and to place feed hoppers or feed stacks with straw to provide something to scratch in such areas. It is also important to work out where they are most likely to stray. They are, for instance, inclined to wander up dry ditches, or along shelter belts, in search of food and may well wander onto neighbouring ground to be lost to the shoot. Such places should then be regularly, but quietly, dogged in towards the main feeding points or release pens on the shoot. By regular feeding and by regular dogging in, even wild birds can be accustomed to a routine. It does not take any bird long to realise that a potential source of regular feeding is available at certain times of the day and the keen rough-shooter will soon notice a considerable increase in the birds on his land.

When it comes to shooting these birds it is important always to remember they will most likely fly towards their feeding points and to avoid, as far as possible, shooting them in the vicinity of their main release pens or favourite feeding and roosting points. If these are unduly disturbed the birds will very probably be driven off the ground. Where there are shelter belts of trees it is comparatively simple for one or two guns with good dogs working well within range to shepherd the birds gently forward until it is desired to flush the birds over waiting guns sited to provide the best shooting on the ground. If there is no convenient cover available but the farmer is interested in improving the shooting, some suitably sited strips of kale planted along the edges of fields will often provide almost as good cover as a strip of trees for the purposes of driving the birds in this way to a good flushing point.

Use of Root Fields

Since their reactions to the approach of danger are very similar, the same principles employed in driving partridges may also be effectively used with pheasants. As with partridges, if the birds can be driven into a field of roots they may then be driven out over waiting guns. Alternatively, the guns may adopt the same circular tactics in the roots as those advocated for partridges, if the root field is felt to be too large for the number of guns to handle it effectively by driving it in strips (see page 60). It will be found, however, that without good dogs working well, old cock pheasants especially are likely to run between the guns in a root field without being flushed. It often requires very good and determined dog work to flush a really experienced old cock pheasant in a root field, especially if they have been driven more than once in the same way. Just as they will quickly learn where the feeding points are, so a wise old bird will quickly learn where his likeliest chance of safety lies.

Shooting Tactics

If a suitable layout can be planned for the shoot (and it must be remembered that many woods throughout the British Isles were laid out towards the end of the last century specifically for shooting) then it is usually possible to move the birds steadily into position before flushing them over the guns to obtain the best possible shooting. Where this state of affairs is non-existent, for instance where there are no trees, different tactics must be employed. If strips of kale or similar cover are not available as a substitute then the ground itself must be studied carefully. It may be that there is a rough grass grown ditch, or dyke, or even more than one, leading to a boggy patch of rush-covered ground. Such conditions are very much favoured by pheasants and there is the bonus that duck, snipe or even woodcock may also be found on the same ground. Alternatively, there may be stubble fields with a valley beyond them over which the birds can be driven and the guns sited below to obtain good shooting. Careful feeding again should help to bring the birds onto the desired ground. Shooting then may be interestingly varied with an exciting bag in prospect.

The Wild Bird in the Open

Although such shooting can provide some exciting moments and some good sport to my mind, it is hard to beat the truly wild bird out in his element on the side of a gorse-covered valley or steep hillside, or even sometimes well out on the moorland shoot. Then the dogs will have to work hard to find him and once up he will fly hard and fast, providing a memorable shot, especially if there is any sort of wind giving him impetus, or curl, in his flight. Such birds may be few and far between, but they are well worth shooting.

In such cases the roughshooter who knows his ground well should be able to tell where the birds are likely to be feeding and at what time of day. It may be, for instance, that the rowan berries have been falling and the birds have been feasting on them. Careful observation of his shoot should have brought any such obvious favoured feeding to his notice. Then, by placing his guns between the birds and their likely line of flight to cover, it is usually possible to hunt the ground and drive some splendid high birds over the guns, providing shots which any gun would be delighted to bring down cleanly. That is the essence of the roughshooter's really wild pheasant.

On the Moorland Shoot

On the edge of a moorland shoot last season just such an opportunity arose when the dogs scented a bird at the foot of a bracken-covered cleft on the edge of the moorland shoot. Following the dogs upwards, the birds were forced up towards the edge of the bracken and the moor. Once in the open they both broke back and, curling downwards across the glen, provided a perfect right and left to my companion remaining below. The pleasure of presenting such a brace of birds intentionally on the roughshoot and the knowledge that one or two such birds may be expected on each outing are enough to enliven any roughshooter's day.

Points on Rearing

It will have already been gathered from the foregoing that unless the roughshooter lives on or very close to the shoot, rearing pheasants on the roughshoot is a difficult if not impossible task. Nor, even if he lives on the ground, are any great numbers normally likely to be reared and released. A hundred or at the most two hundred birds is around the sort of number normal for a roughshoot of say four or five hundred acres. If some forty per cent of those are shot the roughshooter may consider he has done very well indeed. He would probably do better on the whole to invest money on more feeding for the shoot, since the results would probably prove more effective.

On the other hand, if a roughshoot is situated between several other shoots, either driven keepered shoots, or similar roughshoots, which all rear birds, it is only fair that the roughshooter should also try to do his best in this line, rather than simply feed in the hope of attracting other people's birds. Good neighbourliness is part of country life. The keepers on the large estates nearby will look much more kindly on a neighbouring roughshooter who rears some birds and is seen to be attempting to keep down predators and poachers rather than one who simply feeds his boundaries heavily and thus more or less equates himself with the poaching fraternity. There are, after all, ways and ways of poaching and deliberately to entice a neighbour's birds over the boundary, although a very widespread practice, is not one which anyone is likely to look on favourably when they are on the receiving end of it. In such matters it is always well to do as you would be done by. No one likes to think they have expended effort simply for someone else to profit by it.

The Neighbouring Ground

Being on good terms with the neighbours does not only mean being friendly with the keepers of driven shoots in the area, but also with the neighbouring farmers even if they do not shoot. Permission to cross over a boundary in search of a bird, or even to drive in a neighbouring field or woodside strip which will help with the shooting, can often be obtained by asking politely, and the present of a brace of pheasants or some portion of the bag after a shooting day will always be appreciated. Anyone associated with the ground should be invited to shoot, or offered some game occasionally. This can do no harm and its positively beneficial effects on the shooting are likely to be considerable.

If there is a keeper on the boundary rearing birds, the rough-shooter should do his best to get on good terms with him. Even if the roughshooter is unable to rear birds the fact that he is snaring foxes and setting traps for predators should be made plain. It may be that once he is on good terms with the keeper, he will be invited to beat. If he has time this can be both instructive and interesting. If the roughshooter has a well trained dog, or dogs, he may be invited to pick up which can be both interesting and rewarding with the opportunity of watching his dog perform some satisfying dog work as well as being useful and getting some good training in steadiness. Apart from the opportunity to see how the neighbouring land is shot, there is usually on most shoots an organised driven day on cocks at the end of the season for the beaters, tenants and helpers, which can often mean very good sport and an enjoyable day.

The Benefits

Quite apart from the common-sense of being on good terms with the neighbours, both large and small, it can often be that this not only results in better shooting but also in lasting friendships. The neighbour to whom the brace of pheasants is given in return for permission to walk on his side of the hedge as well as your own may eventually extend the invitation to shoot over the whole farm once he sees it is not going to be abused. The keeper aware of the difficulty in overseeing a release pen may offer help, or even possibly a few spare poults. Certainly either acquaintance may result in pigeon and rabbit shooting days apart from many good shared moments of pleasure and many an interesting conversation. In addition, being on good terms with everyone around the shoot will result in losing fewer pheasants. Those roadside poachers who stop their car and shoot a silenced .22 out of the window at the cock pheasant sunning itself in the growing corn will have their number taken by a keen-eyed local and, although you may not even be within miles, the police may well be informed and a court case result.

The Importance of Vigilance

In return, of course, it is important that you note any cars parked on your ground. They may be innocent lovers, or a family out for a picnic, or they may have more sinister intentions and are using your ground as a base to attack your neighbour's release pens. It is always worth noting the number, make and colour of any suspicious looking cars seen in the neighbourhood when attending to trap rounds or supervising the roughshoot in similar ways. If you hear any shots, or have good reason to suspect that poaching is taking place, then a call to the police station will be appreciated. The country police in most areas are very happy to co-operate in catching poachers.

Poachers

The modern poacher sniping from a car with a silenced .22, or sneaking around with a cross-bow with telescopic sights, is a menace. Pheasants are one of their aims, but more often it is deer, which too often are merely wounded and left to die later in agony. Alternatively, they are perfectly capable of shooting a sheep regardless of whether it is an in-lamb ewe about to give birth, perhaps just heedless of the damage and misery they are causing. Some of these mindless lunatics will shoot at anything and there have been hideous cases of horses and ponies, or sheep and cows, wounded by bullets, or crossbow bolts, or sometimes just deliberately slashed with knives and similar weapons in roadside fields. Anyone connected with the countryside must be revolted by barbarous behaviour of this kind and if the roughshooter helps to prevent anything of this nature he will have made friends for life of the locals.

Shooting Days

The question of when to shoot pheasants is sometimes a slightly knotty one for the roughshooter. If he waits until the leaf is off the trees in November then, of course, he will have much more sporting birds. By then, however, many of his pheasants may have strayed for alternative feeding elsewhere. Much must depend on the ground. If there is quite a lot of good holding cover and trees, then clearly waiting until the leaf is off in November and shooting sporting birds must be the correct solution. The November and December birds besides will be full grown and able to fly well, thus presenting a more difficult shot, which is all to the good. The wild moorland birds, however, might only be seen once in October and are better shot when the chance presents itself for a sporting shot. It must be up to the roughshooter to decide, dependent on the ground and local conditions.

Back End Cocks

Some sportsmen advocate shooting the cock birds early in the season before they have learned to slip into cover at the sound of the gun, and there is something to be said for this. On the other hand, the roughshooter may have some good sport walking up the hedgerows for surplus back-end cocks when the frost begins to harden. Then they are likely to be found in the hedgerows, and a gun either side may have good sport.

Driven Pheasants

The truth of the matter is, however, that walked-up pheasants rarely give good or worthwhile shooting, especially in roots or on flat low ground. Unless they can be pushed up in conditions which make for testing shooting they are not likely to provide very much in the way of sporting shooting. Therefore, especially if the roughshooter has reared his own birds, it is highly desirable to organise a driven day whenever possible. Even if this only means using volunteer beaters to drive the birds over the roughshooters and their guests it is worth organising. It is then that the ground must be used in the most imaginative way possible to try to provide sporting shooting.

Coming out of a wood over the treetops in something of a wind with their tails streaming as they curve over the guns, pheasants can provide as testing shooting as any birds. Shot when they are young and still barely full grown, or when soaking wet and barely able to fly out of wet roots, it is hardly worth expending the cartridge. If time and trouble have been spent in rearing birds, or even in simply feeding to attract them, and trapping the predators, it is short-sighted not to try to present them in as challenging a way as the ground and circumstances will allow. Otherwise it seems to me one might just as well shoot them on the ground, or net them, or club them over the head in the pens. The birds should be reared to maturity and encouraged to live in the wild and adapt to it, otherwise there is no point in rearing them in the first place. Only then, when they are free flying wild birds, are they worth shooting.

Put-and-Take Shooting

The principle of put-and-take shooting, like put-and-take fishing, where the fish are reared and placed in the water immediately prior to being caught is surely anathema to any real sportsman. It is practised frequently in parts of the U.S.A. I have had sportsmen visiting me who have explained to me how it is done. The bird is taken from a pen and released under a bush, or thrown into long grass from a Landrover. The shooter, who is paying so many dollars per bird, then comes up with a dog hired for the day. The dog comes on point and the bird is flushed. It is then shot and retrieved, but even should the shooter miss with both barrels the bird will still come down just the same and is still retrieved. The explanation for this is that though it has not been shot the wretched bird, having been in a half-acre pen all its life, is unable to fly any further. Any half-competent retriever can then retrieve it. This, of course, is not sport and should never be tolerated. Indeed, in the U.K. it is prob-ably illegal, being on a par with releasing trap pigeons.

Sport on the Roughshoot

It should not be necessary to point out that unless the quarry has a sporting chance no one with any pretensions to being a sportsman should consider shooting it. On the roughshoot the greatest sat-isfaction and genuine pleasure of shooting should be that this is akin to hunting in the wild. The roughshooter and his dog should be pitting themselves against the natural cunning and instinctive reac-tions of the beast in the wild. To handicap that quarry or to shoot something that has never learned to adapt properly to the ways of the wild is simply neither sporting nor satisfying. Hence it should be unnecessary to point out that reared pheasants should be given every chance to grow to full maturity before the roughshooter should consider shooting them. Anything else is bordering on the unsporting and may even be straightforward butchery. Why not just buy a pound or two of sausages instead?

6

Wildfowl on the Roughshoot

THE MALLARD: *Anas platyrhynchos*

The mallard, *Anas platyrhynchos*, is well-known by sight to almost everyone. The male with his glossy green head, yellow bill, white collar round the neck and purple browny chest with pale grey underparts, and the mottled brown female with orange legs and green bill are to be seen in most public parks and rivers throughout the country. The drake is on average 23 inches from beak to tail and weighs around $2\frac{1}{2}$ lbs while the female is slightly smaller. Their quacking call is also well-known but the variations from a welcoming mutter to a loud feeding shout, or a parting cry of alarm as they take flight on the approach of danger, are a different matter and require studying to understand and imitate effectively.

Mallard are monogamous and pair from January to February, nesting from February to March onwards, usually close by a river or marsh, or at least with access to water, although sometimes surprisingly far from the nearest obvious source. I have even known them nest half-way up a hillside far from any water supply. The nest may be quite a large affair with from eight to ten eggs. They will feed on grain, well-rotted potatoes and young grass, or growing corn inland, and are surface feeders in water, dabbling for grubs, weeds and other natural feed.

THE TEAL: *Anas crecca*

The next commonest duck is probably the Teal, *Anas crecca,* at 14 inches from beak to tail the smallest European duck. The male has a conspicuous chestnut head with a horizontal white stripe and a curving green eye patch and grey speckled underparts. The female is speckled brown and buff, but both have a bright green wing patch. They are quite vocal birds, making a sort of chuckling sound when feeding. Usually found flying in flocks, these are difficult little birds to shoot and make very good eating as well as providing excellent sporting shooting.

Other Wildfowl

There are several other varieties of wildfowl which may be encountered and shot on the roughshoot, depending largely on its whereabouts. Near to the coast, of course, wildfowl are likely to be more varied than on roughshoots far inland. Widgeon, Gadwall, Golden Eye, Pintail, Shoveller and Tufted Duck are amongst the various other ducks the roughshooter may come across and which may be included in his bag if he is lucky. It may also be that he has a shoot visited by geese. In that case he may be fortunate enough to include Canada, Greylag or Pinkfeet geese in his bag at times. If the roughshoot is well placed and near a good wildfowling area the variety of wildfowl and the sport obtained from them may be very considerable. A small flight pond within easy flight of the sea is likely to be well worth feeding regularly and may provide most interesting sport, more especially when the birds are seeking shelter from rough weather. On the whole, however, the mallard is likely to prove the roughshooter's main quarry since it is likely to be found anywhere. Since it is also easily enough reared it may be regarded as the commonest duck shot on the average roughshoot.

Water Supplies

Any roughshoot which has a little water on it should attract wildfowl of various kinds, whether a lake, a small pond, even small rainwater splashes here and there, a length of watery dyke or ditch, a small stream or better still a length of river, especially with water meadows. Wildfowl have even been known to flight into plastic sheeting laid down to simulate water. They will, of course, also flight into stubble fields, or better still laid corn fields. They will also flight in to feed in fields where the potato crop has been lifted and the remains of the crop are to be found rotting on the ground. Finally, geese will often flight into fields of young winter wheat or grass either for grazing or for rest. In short, one way or another, the roughshooter should be fairly certain of some shots at wildfowl of various kinds during the season even on an almost totally dry upland shoot.

Rearing Mallard

If the roughshoot has any promising water supply the chances of wildfowl shooting are considerable. As with pheasant, duck are quite easy to breed and release. If a small lake exists on the roughshoot it is no great problem to rear some duck and release them. Incubating, hatching and rearing to eight weeks or so is easy enough. It is the usual practice then to pen them for a week or so at the edge of the water where they are to be released in order to acclimatise them to the area, but it is important to have the predators, especially mink and foxes, under control. Since they are greedy birds it is not difficult to keep them on the spot. The real problem is to encourage them to take to the wild and fend for themselves. If any quantity are reared and released on a flight pond they will tend to stay in position and eat up all the feed placed to attract wild birds. They may even see off the wild birds.

The difficulty is to force them to take to a life in the wild and not swing round over the waiting guns in a compact group of 'tame' birds. If they can be released on one pond and fed on another, or fed gradually further inland and then chased off their feed to force them to fly by themselves, they may be successfully turned out into the wild. Of course the ratio of birds shot may not be high, but shooting half-tame birds is not something any sportsman would contemplate. The same restrictions on shooting reared mallard must exist as with reared pheasants. Until they are fully grown and flighting into the wild it is both unfair and unreasonable to shoot them. To see a raft of reared mallard take off from a lake and flight back over the guns several times before finally being driven off by sustained volleys is not sport but plain assassination.

Put-and-Take Wildfowl

The same mid-west Americans who told me of the 'put-and-take' pheasant shooting they organised, also described their 'put-and-take' duck slaughter, for it can be called nothing else. The ducks are trained to walk several hundred yards or so from their rearing pond for feeding. The distance is increased each day and they are then trained to ride up a hay elevator and fly back to their pond from the top of it. Come the shooting season, the guns placed in the hides in front of the elevator pay the most for the first shots and progressively behind them the other guns pay less. With the duck shooters in their hides the ducks are then called to slaughter. A Scotswoman I know was invited to one such battue. To her amazement a lame duck, obviously victim of a previous battue and unable to fly, waddled past her and her 'guide' urged her to shoot it.

'If anyone shoots that duck,' she said firmly, 'I will shoot him.'

Such shooting of reared birds is not sport by any standards and is probably illegal in the U.K., but wildfowl which have bred in the wild in their natural surroundings and are shot in normal sporting circumstances can give enormous satisfaction to any shooting man. It is also only fair if numbers of duck are shot during the shooting season that, if possible, some should be returned to the wild. Therefore while it is desirable that some mallard should be reared on the roughshoot, if possible, the aim should be to ensure that they fly free and are not shot in an unsporting fashion.

Feeding a Flight pond

The feeding of a flight pond should bring duck in without any great difficulty. A couple of Khaki Campbells will act as call duck if desired, but usually they will not be necessary. Well-sited duck flighting ponds, regularly fed, will attract duck with little problem. The best feeding for this purpose is the tailings from a corn drier if these are available. These coarse ears of corn with a few grains left in them are ideal to attract wildfowl as they float on the surface and are easily seen by passing duck. The place to feed the pond is in the shallows, where it is about six inches to a foot deep. Duck thoroughly enjoy paddling on the surface and diving down for their feed. Well-rotted potatoes and corn scattered around are also welcome feeding.

Building a Flight pond

Where the roughshoot is without any flight pond but there is a suitable site available, it is an easy matter to construct one. It is simply a question of scooping out a small flight pond with a hired digger in the chosen place where there is a supply of water available. Some reeds and quick growing shrubs should be grown round the edges and with a little feed provided should prove an effective draw for wildfowl.

It may be necessary to line the pond with heavy PVC if the surface is unsuitable for holding water. It is then desirable to lay a soft bed of sand over the surface to prevent the PVC being punctured by sharp stones. It should also be covered with soil, or sunlight may cause it to crack and leak after a year or so. It will, in any event, be advisable to fence off the pond with barbed wire if stock are likely to be around as they can turn such a pond into a mire in no time and may well eat feed such as potatoes or corn and possibly die as a result. They will also almost certainly damage any hides which may have been erected round the pond, so on all counts it is desirable to protect it well. It is also desirable if possible to have a source of running water, whether a spring, or stream, providing both inflow and outflow to prevent the surface from freezing as readily in hard weather. On the other hand, care is necessary to make sure that too much through flow does not cause undue silting.

Feeding a Lake or River

The question of feeding is all important on a river or larger patch of water where the duck may come in at several points. If the roughshoot has a stream, or river, the best method is to feed it at convenient bends so that the duck will come down at selected spots. It should then be possible to stalk the river upwind, and, on a windy day especially, a few mallard may be shot at each bend in turn. On a still day, of course, the whole lot may be alarmed and depart at the first shots; the only chance then is to site several guns on the line the duck are likely to take when flushed. In general, however, on a roughshoot with a river or stream, this method will provide a good deal of regular sport.

Even a broad ditch or dyke may well be attractive to wildfowl and here again there are likely to be patches, especially where a field drain or another ditch joins it, where wildfowl find regular feeding.

By supplementing such places with regular feeding they are almost certain to be sure of some wildfowl each roughshooting day. This is generally the sort of place where a few hours with a digger will provide a useful flight pond if the farmer or landowner is agreeable.

Feeding a Lake

On a larger patch of water it is necessary to study the prevailing winds and the small inlets where wildfowl delight to settle and feed on insects, floating berries and other food which has drifted into them. By feeding these small places, as with the river, it is possible to have some good sport stalking these various points on a rough-shooting day. Where there is only one pond or lake available, however, it is as well to shoot it at the start of the day, before the duck are disturbed by shooting elsewhere. The duck will then have plenty of time to return for the evening flight. In some cases they may return before then so that a second attempt may be made to shoot it before flighting.

Points on Shooting

As a matter of principle it is advisable never to overdo the shooting of any pond or other site. Once a fortnight is usually quite enough. Any more than this and the birds will be driven away. On the other hand, a good day should always be chosen if possible. It is for instance absurd to wait for wildfowl to flight in on an absolutely calm day with no wind. It is always desirable, even when flighting ducks into stubble fields, to have a good breeze at least.

When one of a pair of mallard is bagged during the day on a river or lake and the other flies off, it is well worth returning within a hour or so for the chances are very high that the other will have returned to look for its companion and a careful approach may result in a full brace in the bag. In any event, when duck of any kind are driven off water it is always worth reloading at once if the gun has been fired and freezing in position, going down on one knee beside the nearest bush or any other cover handy and waiting for the ducks to turn and flight over. They will often fly over well within range and provide very testing shooting if they have any sort of wind behind them.

Hide Building

Building hides for duck flighting can be a matter of a few seconds or the work of many hours. If a hide is wanted in a stubble field it may be made from a sixteen or so small oblong easily-handled bales. Probably the easiest and best hide to erect is a square, up to head height, with an opening at one side, since even in the middle of the field it will not worry the incoming birds unduly. Like pigeons, they are accustomed to seeing bales in harvest fields and pay very little attention to them. Otherwise, a length of camouflage netting and some light steel supports stuck firmly into the ground can make an instant hide almost anywhere.

For a more permanent but readily constructed hide a few broken wooden pallets – used on most farms for transporting fertiliser bags and similar sacks on forklifts – can be easily assembled into a fairly sheep- and cattle-proof hide with the aid of a fence post driven into the ground at each corner. A few reeds or rushes interwoven into this may be helpful, but they are often grazed off by cattle or sheep who think it is some sort of special feeding arrangement laid out for their benefit. Left in position for a few days, the duck will soon get used to the hide and come in and feed quite happily in front of it.

Inland Wildfowling

As indicated, mallard and teal are the main duck that the inland wildfowler is likely to encounter, but occasional visitors such as tufted duck and shoveller may be driven inland in hard weather; golden eye, pintail and even the occasional widgeon may also be encountered, depending on how far away the nearest coastline is to be found. Geese may also be seen in many parts of the country and are often found in upland moorland farms resting contentedly enough away from harassment and possibly eating the long coarse grass.

GEESE

For many years I used to have geese coming down on a low ground shoot and encouraged them to do so by only shooting them about once a season. Since they knew they had a fairly safe sanctuary they would fly off if disturbed but soon return, not just in twenties and thirties but in groups of several hundred. It was a great pleasure simply listening to them, but naturally the neighbouring farmers did not enjoy having their young corn eaten and trampled by them. There is no doubt that in large numbers they can do a lot of damage.

In such cases they are easily decoyed. Rising before dawn and setting out decoys in a likely spot near the hide should be enough to bring the geese in. If you are expert enough to call them in well and good but if in doubt leave the calling to someone else since it is easy to give an alarm call if you do not know what you are about.

Decoys for Geese

There are several kinds of decoy available, and the simple cardboard silhouettes are probably as good as any. The only problem with them, if any sort of wind is blowing, is that they do tend to take off and chasing after them in the uncertain light of dawn is not conducive to bringing in geese. Good small groupings are advisable, leaving a gap between two groups, which look both inviting and safe to any approaching skein. Securely hidden in a ditch or hide, the waiting guns should let them come well within range before firing.

Importance of Swing and Aim

Although geese are a large target it is amazing how many people become hypnotised by their size and do not swing fast enough. They rise just about twice as fast as one would expect. As soon as they see danger they can swerve and rise with amazing rapidity. If aim is taken at the head and neck of an individual goose and the gun is swung well through it should fall dead. When geese are within reasonable range there is no real reason for not having a right and left. The fact is that many people become excited at a shot they do not see often and simply tighten up and start poking, missing behind or, worse still, wounding the bird.

While many self-styled experts advocate three inch magnums and full choked guns loaded with AAA or even heavier shot, I am sure that the real secret is to get well within range of the geese. This can admittedly often be a difficult task on the foreshore where cowboy optimists armed with three inch magnum 12 bores, or even 8 bores, are saluting geese far out of range. Whether they are wounding the poor beasts or not they are certainly making sure they will not come within range of anyone else. In inland wildfowling, however, the roughshooter should not suffer this handicap.

An old friend of mine, expert shot with rifle and shotgun, went wildfowling on the Tay once. He went with an experienced wild-fowler as guide to the foreshore. The geese came in over them and he shot six rights and lefts using six shot in improved cylinder and half choke ordinary 12 bore barrels. He then decided it was too easy and never shot geese again. Admittedly he was a man who had as much driven shooting as he wished, shooting sometimes six days a week during the season. He was a superlative shot and I saw him on more than one occasion take every bird in a drive right and left. Even so, his reaction to wildfowling was somewhat excessive. However, a dozen geese do make quite a large pile and one can see his point.

This does, however, make it plain that straight shooting is more important than heavy loads and large guns. The fact is that few people bother to plate their guns with heavy loads and many would find to their surprise that the gun loaded with AAA gives a very poor pattern indeed, as large as a barn door at forty yards with gaps through which half a dozen geese could fly. The net result is wounded geese and a demoralised shooter who takes ever wilder shots. Had he stuck to a weight of shot, no heavier than BB at most, that suited his gun and ensured the geese were within range he would probably have killed cleanly and had a satisfactory day.

Other Reasons for Missing Wildfowl

Another reason for many misses at wildfowl is that the greater part of this shooting takes place in wet and cold conditions when the shooter is wearing far more clothes than is normally his wont. The result is that his gun does not come up as easily as it usually does. He finds it difficult to aim and swing and the result is a miss behind, or a wounded bird. If you find that you need to wear extra clothing, make sure that the gun you are using fits properly. Half an inch or more off the butt might make all the difference, but of course if you have only one gun you must compromise. Wear several fine layers of underclothing which does not make for bulk but does make for warmth and leave those great heavy sweaters behind. Above all make sure you can raise your gun easily and swing freely. It is amazing how many people hamper themselves in this way and then wonder why they miss.

Yet another reason for missing wildfowl is the fact that frequently the shooter has been lying for some time in a very cramped and uncomfortable position, kneeling perhaps in a frozen hole or ditch.

His muscles are cramped and, unused to shooting from a sitting position, he simply does not swing fast enough. The answer is always to try to keep the muscles flexing while you wait and always to try to stand up and take a normal swing if you can. Easier said than done in most cases, but the sport will be much better if it is possible to swing freely.

At the Start of the Season

As with almost every other form of shooting it is also necessary to accustom oneself to wildfowl shooting at the start of each season. Just as grouse are different from partridges and shooting either is very different from shooting pheasants, so wildfowl shooting requires its own expertise. Also, as with each gamebird, those shot early in the season differ vastly from the same birds later in the year.

The early mallard shot in September, while still recovering from the moult, known descriptively as 'flappers', are sometimes so slow in taking to flight that they may often be retrieved by a dog if it is a powerful swimmer. Once they have fully recovered from the moult, however, they rise swiftly from the water and it is essential to swing right through the bird and shoot well above it or it will be missed below. This, of course, applies even more to springing teal which, being a smaller mark, often seem to be shot behind. Surprisingly, however, geese, like blackgame, though bulky and apparently clumsier can rise even faster and more must be missed below by wildfowlers crawling up on them than almost any other bird.

Flighting into Stubble Fields

At around harvest time it is often possible to have good sport waiting for birds flighting into stubble fields or laid corn. As with pigeon shooting, reconnaissance is all-important and it is necessary to know where they are feeding. In laid corn, of course, they can do a lot of damage and the traces of their presence are fairly obvious. The best method of shooting them in such circumstances is to find the flight lines, if these can be established, and to shoot them as they approach the fields, rather than as they are actually coming in to land. In this way the same patch of feeding may be used on more than one occasion to good effect.

Decoys for Duck

The use of decoys to attract mallard to a flight pond should be similar to that advocated for geese. It is desirable to have two groups, heads all pointing roughly into the wind and anchored to allow them to bob with the water in a lifelike manner. Quite a useful arrangement if it is possible to carry the bulk required is to secure four mallard decoys to a light wooden cross. It is important that they all point roughly in the right direction and that the wood does not show above the surface. With a lead weight and cord holding this in position it is possible to place eight mallard decoys in a lifelike group with the minimum of arrangements and know that they will stay in position. The worst of placing decoys individually in position in water is that very often one gets upset and bobs about in a most unnatural way like a toy duck in a bath. Nor is it always possible to see when this happens and the moment of realisation only dawns as the second lot of mallard coming in veer suddenly upwards out of range.

As with any type of decoy it is important that they are painted in flat matt colours. Bright glaring artificial colours reflecting the light are enough to put off any bird. Some of the decoys one sees are also not particularly lifelike, but in general if they will float reasonably they should be successful enough. The making of decoys, of course, is an art even older than shooting. The North American Indians make decoys with mud and feathers which bring in birds and the old fowlers' solid wood-carved decoys are now prized antiques as well as being for the most part works of art. The main objection to solid decoys, of course, is merely their weight and bulk. If access to the pond is at all difficult it is quite a task carrying a load of decoys, even when they are lightweight modern dummies.

Waiting in the Hide

Whenever waiting for duck to flight into a pond it must be impressed on everyone that faces are not raised at the sound of duck wings overhead. The first comers, as every experienced wildfowler knows, will often circle round several times, especially if suspicious, or if there is very little wind. Then it is important to remain still and not start swinging the gun in the hope of getting off a shot, or looking round the sky eagerly to get a glimpse of them. They will be the first to spot suspicious movement, the glint of gun barrels raised in the half-light, or a blur of white face staring up at them. Any of these are enough to cause them to fly on to a neighbouring pond where there may be other fowlers waiting for them who are less impatient and whose experience pays off.

As well as making sure that no one shoots too soon, or moves around in their hide, it is often advisable to arrange beforehand how the guns will fire, depending on how the birds are flighting in. Thus if the guns are placed in three separate hides in line it may be desirable for the first gun to let the birds pass him before firing or the other two may not get any shooting at all. With satisfactory restraint in these matters usually all the guns should have an equal share of the shooting.

The Placing of the Hides and Safety

It is difficult to make any hard and fast rules about how the hides should be placed since much depends on the situation and shape of the flight pond itself. It is, however, always important to ensure that there is no possibility of the guns firing any dangerous shots. It is important that each knows where the other hides are placed and from which directions the duck are most likely to come. Everyone should have been well briefed on such points before the flight has started so that the best shooting may be had by all concerned and there is no possibility of dangerous shots being fired.

It is also important that dogs are kept under control. Usually it is not desirable to let them go for a retrieve until the flight is over, when either the duck have ceased to come in or it is agreed that it is too dark to see and time to pack up for the night. The effect of a wild dog splashing round the pond in pursuit of wounded duck, while its master whistles or shouts in vain should be enough to put off any incoming duck. It is true I have known duck coming in even in these circumstances, but it is clearly not desirable. On the other hand if a duck is flapping round the water it is sometimes desirable to send a steady dog in to fetch it before the flight is over, since it may well put off incoming duck. It is a question of balancing the odds, and if a quick retrieve can be more or less guaranteed that is possibly the best option.

Waiting for the Flight

There may sometimes be quite a long wait for the duck to flight. During this time it is interesting to watch the movements of the wildlife and listen to the sounds they make as they prepare for the night. The crows and rooks returning to roost flapping noisily overhead are amongst the familiar sights. The sound of cock pheasants giving a strident 'Cock-up, cock-up' as they fly up noisily to roost is also very common. The whirring of a covey of partridges crossing a hedge to jug in a stubble field may also be heard occasionally. The almost silent flight of snipe or woodcock as the darkening approaches may be just visible and a shot even be possible. The splashing of moorhens attacking the feed may make the listener think duck have arrived, but the first whicker of wings overhead is not easily missed.

One thing which should never be allowed while waiting for duck is smoking. The sight of a glowing cigarette end or pipe bowl, or a stream of tobacco smoke, is enough to put off any self-respecting duck. I know plenty of people who find it difficult to do without a puff or two at a pipe or cigarette during a lengthy wait for wildfowl to flight in, but it simply should not be permitted.

After the Flight

A powerful torch is a useful asset when flighting at night. Although the dogs will probably have picked all the duck down it is as well to be able to see what you are about. When holding a duck by the body the head should hang down if it is dead. If it remains stretched out it is still alive and may well take off when placed in the gamebag. Many a so-called dead duck has disappeared from the gamebag in such circumstances. When a duck is wounded and on land it will always make for the nearest water. If a wounded duck lands in water it will make for land, but in rushes or deep water it may dive to the bottom and never be recovered. It is important to count the duck down and try to account for them all.

Limiting the Bag

Whether flighting wildfowl at dawn or dusk a decent limit should always be drawn. There are times, perhaps only once or twice in a lifetime, and certainly not common even in the keenest wildfowler's experience, when the birds keep coming regardless. It may be that hard weather has brought them in, although shooting has not yet been stopped by law. Or it may just be one of those days when conditions have conspired to bring them in to that particular spot. Do not then just go on shooting mindlessly. Set a limit to your bag of ten or fifteen, or whatever. Anything more than that is unnecessary. Leave them to come again another day. Restraint is always necessary with a loaded gun.

After the Day is Over

One last point on wildfowling on the roughshoot: if you have been flighting late in freezing weather and the shot birds and decoys have all been collected, remember that this is not the end of the affair. After you have distributed such ducks as you are going to pass on as gifts to the farmer or others who may help on the shoot, and once the game has been hung up properly in the game larder, but before you have cleaned and dried your gun, the first thing to do is to look after your dog. He should be dried and fed and left kennelled and warm. Only then should the gun be cleaned, dried and oiled. After that the roughshooter can treat himself to a warming drink and stretch his legs before the fire prior to a good warm bath and a meal. First things first and the dog that provides you with sport should receive your first attention on your return home.

7

Pigeons on the Roughshoot

Whatever type of roughshoot it may be whether moorland or low ground, marshy bog, or woodland, the roughshooter will almost always be able to shoot pigeons. Indeed on many shoots they may well make up the bulk of his sport. In some Forestry Commission shoots for instance they may well be amongst the commonest birds to be found and in other such shoots they may be noticeable by their absence. Too much forestry is no more satisfactory for pigeons than for any other birds, or for wildlife in general, other than foxes and deer.

THE RING NECKED DOVE: *Columba palumbus*

Habits and Habitat

The ideal habitat for the ring necked dove, *Columba palumbus*, the pigeon most frequently encountered in Britain, is a mixed one of varied agriculture combined with small woods and hedges which provide ideal nesting and feeding ground for this omnivorous greedy eater. Wood pigeons, or ring necked doves, will eat almost anything, being particularly fond of green crops such as kale, cabbages, broccoli and peas, but equally happy with newly sown cereal crops and fresh clover. They will also eat grass seeds and insects and virtually any vegetation they can tear with their beak.

The wood pigeon is so common as barely to merit description, yet remarkably few people other than those who have shot them regularly could probably describe it accurately. It is about 16 inches from beak to tail, and weighs from 1–1½ lbs. It has reddy-pinkish legs with a noticeable yellow bill and a marked white lump above the nostrils.

Its blue-grey plumage has a noticeable white patch on either side of the neck and white bands across each wing with a further white patch across the underside of the tail, all very distinct in flight. Their rather harsh repeated call of 'Coo-coo' is widely heard in spring and summer.

Nests

They will nest in a great variety of places, from ground level upwards, but generally around six or ten feet up. The nest itself is usually a fairly crude affair large enough for the adult birds and the normal clutch of two eggs. Although only two eggs are laid at a time the pigeon's incubation period is remarkably short at only seventeen days and they will continue to lay throughout a great part of the year. Both male and female help to incubate the eggs taking it in turns to do so and if the female is killed the male will usually hatch off the eggs and feed the young. They will normally lay around five clutches of eggs, thus the chances are that each adult pair may rear four to eight progeny or more, much depending on the rate of predation and the feeding available.

Principal Predators

Where the game is well preserved and the predators strictly controlled the pigeons will benefit accordingly. In areas of this kind there is likely to be a greater pigeon population because of the absence of predators such as squirrels, crows, stoats and weasels, which are amongst their greatest enemies in the wild. Feral cats and mink are both also likely to make a meal of young pigeons given the chance and, of course, foxes may also account for a few of the young birds before they have learned their parents' natural cunning.

Feeding Habits

What the wood pigeon eats throughout the year will vary with the seasons and with the feeding available. From January to February weeds, the tops of green crops, brassica, thorn and similar berries and clover are likely to be their main diet. In March and April the early shoots of clover, corn and oil seed rape, with weeds, and early growth of peas and beans might well be eaten. In May and June oil seed rape, weeds and clover along with garden or horticultural produce are the main source of supply. In July and August corn, weeds, snails, small insects, peas and oil seed rape are probably the principal feeding, with laid crops a main target whenever available. In September and October they glean the stubbles and any laid crops, or newly drilled corn, and feed on berries from the woods and hedges. In November and December they are likely to be found in the woods searching for beech mast, berries and acorns, or in the fields attacking kale and green crops, as well as the remaining weeds. Thus it can be clearly seen that they have few friends in the farming, horticultural or gardening world. The damage a flock of wood pigeons can do to a field of growing vegetables can amount to total destruction.

Background

The wood pigeon is undoubtedly a pest to gardeners, smallholders and farmers, but on the other hand he is almost entirely a bonus to the roughshooter for he provides sport both in and outside the game shooting season. This nearly ubiquitous bird can also provide extremely tricky and sporting shooting and furthermore may be shot without a game licence. The strange thing is that it was comparatively uncommon as late as the 1840s. The farming boom of the early Victorian period and subsequent slump of the 1860s and 70s resulted in a tremendous increase in shooting and in the keepering of large estates. The net result was that conditions for the wood pigeon to breed were perfect, with its predators mostly killed by gamekeepers and with plentiful feeding almost freely available. The result was a vast increase in their numbers and it was only in the First World War that it was appreciated that they had reached nearly plague proportions and some concerted action was taken against them. The Second World War also resulted in action being taken against them by the government, to the extent that subsidised cartridges were widely available for anyone prepared to shoot them, but they remain a fairly ubiquitous pest to all crop growers as well as a source of sport to the roughshooter.

The Young Bird

The young wood pigeon, or squab, as it is termed is a repulsive-looking object with a wrinkled bluey-grey skin with a thin covering of yellowy hair or down. It has a flat soft grey beak and in the first week or so is fed a soft creamy substance known as crop milk which the parents regurgitate and which the young bird eagerly searches for with its oddly shaped beak. Inside about ten days the hairy down has given way to the juvenile feathers and the beak has begun to resemble the adult shape.

Defence Mechanism

At this stage they have a strange defence mechanism when faced with danger, puffing themselves out like a toad, spreading their wings to increase their size even further and making a fierce hissing sound, while rushing forwards to peck any intruder. They can give a quite surprisingly hard peck and this defence may well be successful in some cases, but against a determined owl or hawk or a hunting rat, weasel, stoat, or polecat they would stand little chance and this is the period when the young are probably at their most vulnerable.

Growth and Predation

The young squab generally leaves the nest after about a month and at around six weeks starts its first moult, which may be checked in winter, so that they continue to look darker grey than the adults. At this intermediate stage they are again prey to numerous predators, such as sparrow hawks and cats, but once they have survived for a month or so they have gained the adult wood pigeon's alertness and cunning.

Alertness and Gregariousness

Few birds are quite as alert to danger as the wood pigeon. This is easily proved by a walk through almost any wood when they will invariably leave a tree between themselves and anyone approaching as they depart with a minor clap of wings and the sound of breaking twigs. The sound of their departure will alert the next bird, and so on. The wood pigeon, however, does have a naturally gregarious disposition. A single bird will always fly in to join a feeding group of birds. They delight in the company of their fellows and it is this trait, of course, which can be usefully exploited by the roughshooter by the use of well placed decoys to encourage the passing birds to come within shot.

THE STOCK DOVE: *Columba oenas*

Apart from domestic pigeons gone feral, which have bred in the wild and now make up one of the largest groups of pigeons likely to be encountered in the U.K. next to wood pigeons, the roughshooter may also encounter stock doves, *Columba oenas*. Only about 13 inches from beak to tail it lacks the wood pigeon's white bars on the neck and wings and is a darker bluey-grey in colour. It also has handsome glossy green patches on either side of the neck, which are clearly visible at close quarters. In flight it has a faster wing beat and appears an altogether dumpier bird. It has a softer call and a shorter less powerful beak better adapted for eating seeds, which constitute a large part of its diet. It is not in general such a destructive nuisance as the wood pigeon, although in large numbers it can still cause considerable damage to crops.

THE ROCK DOVE: *Columba livia*

The stock dove is protected under the 1981 Wildlife and Countryside Act, although if a farmer considers he is suffering damage from excessive numbers eating his crops he may apply for a permit to shoot them, which will usually be granted. Also protected under the same Act with the same proviso is the rock dove, *Columba livia*. Very similar in size to the stock dove it has two clearly-marked black wing bars and a white rump patch, with similar glossy green throat patches to the stock dove. It has similar tastes in food, but as its name implies likes to live in the vicinity of cliffs and quarries, usually flying extremely sharply downwards when disturbed. The true rock dove is now only found in the cliffs of Caithness and Sutherland. Elsewhere it has been replaced by feral escapees, often very similar in appearance and reactions, but with enormous variations in colouring. Under the 1981 Wildlife and Countryside Act these may be shot and may provide very sporting shooting.

THE TURTLE DOVE: *Streptopelia turtur*, and the COLLARED DOVE: *Streptopelia decoacta*

The only two remaining doves likely to be encountered are the turtle dove, *Streptopelia turtur*, a summer visitor which is protected and the rather similar collared dove, *Streptopelia decoacta*, which has rapidly become established in the U.K. since the early 1950s and is now reaching pest proportions in many areas and is rightly no longer protected. Both these birds are only around 11 inches from beak to tail. The turtle dove has browny wings and a black tail with white edges. It has a soft call and is found in orchards and similar country.

The collared dove, as the name implies has a narrow black half collar round its neck. The upper parts are dusty brown with pale grey shoulders, it has red eyes and a short harsh unpleasing call of 'Kaa, kaa, kaa'. It is often found close to buildings and villages. It may cross with the turtle dove and the results are indistinguishable from the collared dove. Although small, the collared dove is good to eat and should be shot at every opportunity. Once they have been shot at they develop a high degree of cunning like their larger cousin the wood pigeon, but it does not require a great deal of shot to deal with them adequately.

RACING PIGEONS

It is illegal and rightly so knowingly to shoot racing pigeons. Breeding racing pigeons is a very expensive business and good racing pigeons may cost hundreds of pounds and upwards. The pigeon shooter should always be careful to avoid making a mistake, but racing birds are rarely encountered when decoying pigeons or flighting wild birds coming in to roost.

Occasionally, however, a ringed bird may be shot, usually amongst a group of feral pigeons, with the breeder's number and date of registration on the ring as permanent evidence of identity. If such a bird is shot the ring should be removed and given to the police or nearest known breeder. A bird which has gone astray for any length of time does not matter, but one killed competing in a race might represent a very considerable loss. It is desirable from the breeder's viewpoint to know of the death of a bird, even if this is only negative information, but the shooter should avoid any mistakes as far as possible and racing pigeons are generally easily enough identified.

Natural Decoys

The use of decoys to exploit the gregarious instincts of pigeons is perhaps the commonest method employed to shoot them. It is illegal to use tethered live birds, but a great deal of time and ingenuity is often spent in devising the most lifelike substitute possible. The decoys used may be of various kinds, but those most commonly used and probably the best are recently shot birds propped up in a lifelike manner with a stick or wire supporting the head. Some people advocate using birds which have been frozen in the deep freeze, others insist on using birds which have been gutted and their flesh preserved with injections of formaldehyde. These are all variants on the actual bird.

Artificial Decoys

There are also numerous artificial decoys manufactured, which may be made from wood, rubber, moulded polymer, plastic and numerous other substances. These may include inflatable decoys and many of them are very effective. There are also flat plastic or stiffened paper decoys, propped on wire or wooden supports, while some enthusiasts use home-made hollow shell dummies, cut-out models of pigeons made from linoleum, tin, or any similar light easily handled material. These are known as 'Max Baker' decoys after their inventor, the first man in the U.K. to write about serious decoying in the 1930s.

All or any of these artificial decoys may at times effectively decoy pigeons, for the fact is that at times pigeons will come in to almost anything of grey and white colouring. It has been suggested they would even come in to heaps of iron filings and one acquaintance of mine has effectively decoyed them in to a flat slate with white chalk markings simulating the patch marks on throat and wings. In the Pyrenees they are decoyed into nets in the mountain passes by throwing a grey and white coloured bat twirling in front of them. Similarly, wing-flapping dummies are often used by keen pigeon shooters to attract passing birds and various models may be purchased in most gunsmiths. The major point about all artificial decoys should be that they are painted in a matt paint and do not shine and catch the light unnaturally. Any such unnatural feature will cause approaching birds to veer away from the decoys rather than come in to them.

Setting Out Decoys

Whatever kind are used the decoys may be set out in groups, or 'rafts', preferably in a horseshoe pattern to provide an inviting gap into which the incoming pigeons are likely to fly. The birds should all be facing roughly into the wind, as would be the case with feeding birds. They should not be set too close together but with about 18 inches between them. They should generally be set out downwind in relation to the pigeon shooter waiting concealed in his hide so that he obtains the best shot possible as they flight into the decoy birds. Within reason the more that can be quickly set out the better.

Lofted Decoys

The decoys are usually more effective if one or two suitably placed lofted decoys can be added to them. These may only be 'lofted' on top of a convenient fence post, but if there is a convenient tree handy, in which a pigeon might be likely to sit, then a bird lofted high in this will probably prove immensely attractive to passing birds and, on swerving to investigate the lofted bird, they will more than probably then flight into the other decoys laid out below if they are invitingly placed.

A light aluminium extending ladder will be found extremely useful for siting such lofted decoys in trees. With the aid of the ladder and a lengthy cane pole it is usually possible to place such a decoy facing into the wind in the upper branches of a tree where it may be seen by pigeons passing over a wide area. Trying to loft decoys by other methods often advocated, such as a sweep's set of extending rods, an arrow or a cricket ball attached to a line, or using a casting rod, are all liable to end in tangles and frayed tempers unless the tree is unusually easily approached. A ladder is easily enough carried on a roof rack and may prove an extremely useful asset at times.

Watching the Reactions of Flighting Birds

When waiting in the hide with the decoys spread out in front of him the shooter should study the reactions of the birds coming in to them. If they flight straight in without hesitation then clearly all is well and there is nothing wrong with the decoys. If it is noticeable that the birds are starting to come in then veering away abruptly it can mean either they have seen the pigeon shooter in his hide, or there is something wrong with the way the decoys have been set out. If the pigeon shooter is certain there is nothing wrong with his hide and is sure he has made no obvious movement which may have caused the birds to be suspicious and if the same thing happens again, he is well advised to investigate the decoys to see what may be wrong with them.

It may be that some have fallen over and are obviously unnatural. Some on the other hand may not be pointing upwind, or may be placed too close together or in an unnatural position. Or there may be too many feathers showing from the last pigeons shot, or something obviously unnatural which the approaching birds have seen as a warning. Until it is corrected the pigeon shooter is likely to have little success.

The Wrong Place

It may just be, of course, that the pigeon shooter has chosen the wrong place and the pigeons are intent on feeding elsewhere, even if only a matter of a hundred yards or so further down a field. It could be that when prospecting the ground through binoculars he mistook his bearings and chose the wrong spot. It could be that the pigeons have moved further on to feed. Whatever the reason, there is no future in remaining in one place when it is clear the pigeons are feeding elsewhere. It is wise on such occasions to admit your mistake and move elsewhere, rather than spend a fruitless few hours in the wrong place and shoot nothing.

The Hide

The hide itself may be on several levels. A good hide may often be placed below ground level in a convenient ditch, or even in a hole specifically dug for the purpose. The pigeon shooter thus placed may well have good shooting and be invisible to approaching birds. Otherwise it may be that a convenient hide can be erected by a fence, or alongside some agricultural machinery, beneath a tree, bush, or straw stack, or similar place. The hide may even be made of sixteen or so straw bales, or from plastic netting covered with dyed hessian to resemble a large round straw bale.

Such hides may be semi-permanent, being built at the beginning of the season for use throughout the year if required, or made specifically for the occasion. With the aid of a billhook and some metal supports a hide can be readily constructed with the aid of some branches cut from elder or broom, or similar sources. It is important, however, not to damage growing trees or hedgerows and permission to build such hides should always be asked beforehand.

At Treetop Level

On a different level superb sport can sometimes be obtained by siting a hide on top of a straw stack, or at treetop level, when the birds may be shot as they flight in. More often, however, a treetop platform hide is used for roost shooting, or flighting birds in passage. Many shoots will have a clearly marked passage, or flight line, which pigeons follow from one feeding ground or roost to another at intervals more or less continuously throughout the day. A hide set on such flight lines may provide tremendous sport at times and will almost always have a regular supply of pigeons flighting over it at intervals. To test the value and suitability of treetop platforms an aluminium ladder is again invaluable. Furthermore, it may be used as a means of access so that no unauthorised people can use these platforms.

Flighting

Flighting birds coming in to roost in the evening can be very good sport, from ground level or from a platform, but from a platform it equals almost any other form of shooting. The birds will be coming from all angles at the level of the gun, or below, or flighting in from above. With any sort of wind they are likely to be curling birds, providing the most testing of shooting. This is undoubtedly amongst the most interesting forms of pigeon shooting and the average of shots to kills is likely to be very poor at times for even the finest of shots.

Passage Birds

On many roughshoots there will be one or more lines regularly taken by pigeons flighting between two points, either to feed or roost, or following a natural contour of the ground between two points. It can often be worth placing a semi-permanent hide on the line of such passage birds, which may provide regular sport. Such flight lines, of course, are liable to change from time to time with a change in the feeding habits and the time of year. Regularly used lines of this nature can, however, often provide good sport.

Quarry Shooting

Another very sporting as well as testing form of pigeon shooting can be had in quarries. Feral birds roosting in quarries can often provide extremely testing shooting in the same way as with platform shooting. Here the need for a head for heights is sometimes required. Shooting downwards it is easy to get an attack of vertigo as the birds swing abruptly downwards and a bird may be shot at full range beneath your feet. In a very different way, birds coming over the quarry edge in a group may split into swerving, curving targets all going different ways in an instant. This is as hard as any driven partridge coming over a high East Anglian hedge and makes for very testing sport.

Clifftop Shooting

Yet again the roughshooter may be fortunate in having some clifftop shooting available. This too can be a very testing form of pigeon shooting. With one gun on the clifftops and one below the feral birds can prove extremely challenging shooting, sometimes exploding abruptly downwards and at other times coming over the edge of the cliff and upwards like bullets.

The roughshooter with his own cliff edge to the sea is a rarity, but he should have good sport, both on pigeons and on rabbits. It is advisable to have a tide table and a walkie-talkie radio for communication between guns above and below for it does not pay to get caught by the tides and it is as well to have warnings of overhangs and unsafe places. This is one time when reconnaissance of the ground beforehand is certainly not wasted and until he knows his ground thoroughly the prospective pigeon shooter should have considerable care.

Use of Binoculars and Map

In all forms of pigeon shooting the old army saying, 'Time spent on reconnaissance is seldom wasted' could not be more true. Firstly the roughshooter would-be pigeon shooter should know his ground intimately, both on the ground and from a map. He should know in which fields crops are growing which are likely to be of interest to wild pigeons. He will supplement this knowledge by going out on the ground with a pair of good binoculars and looking out for signs of feeding birds. Next he will work out from which main direction these birds are coming and which parts of the field they seem to be most interested in. He will then be able to site his hide, or hides if he has a companion, and his decoys so as to attract the pigeons within range of his gun.

If he has done his homework in advance the roughshooter will already know which are the main roosting woods and assembly points in an area covering several miles around his shoot. He will also know where the main crops are sited which are likely to be of interest to them. By shooting a few pigeons on the flight lines and examining their crops he may find them crammed at various times with say cabbage leaves, beech mast or clover and will be able to pinpoint almost exactly where they have been feeding. In this way he will be able to go to the right place and set out his hides and decoys, if he has not already laid on semi-permanent hides on the spot, and be fairly certain of some sport to come.

Two or More Guns

Although pigeon shooting tends to be regarded as a sport for the lone shooter, in practice two or more can have good sport dependent on the circumstances and the ground. As already noted, clifftop shooting requires one gun below and one above and the same can often be true of quarry shooting, when one gun below can keep the birds on the move and the gun or guns above may have fairly continuous sport as the birds come in to roost in the rocky ledges. In the same way at roosting time two or more guns placed round a wood may have very good sport.

Too many guns may cause the birds to desert a roosting wood, but two or three are not likely to do so, and a wood of this kind on a roughshoot can prove a source of steady sport throughout the year. In addition, of course, good sport may be had walking up a woodland area divided by rides. By taking the rides separately according to a prearranged plan it is often possible to keep birds moving and obtain a great deal of shooting as the birds flight across the rides, uncertain where the danger lies. This form of shooting may result in quite large bags and surprisingly good sport. It may be desirable, however, as in clifftop shooting, for the pigeon shooters to be in touch by walkie-talkie since it is easy to lose touch with each other and the pace may vary considerably as one or other halts to send his dog to pick up a bird fallen inside the wood.

Use of Echoes and Bangers

It is always worthwhile a roughshooter noting wherever he finds an echo on the shoot, for it can often pay to exploit this. The birds hearing a shot echo back from a cliff or hillside may well flight towards the original source of the shot and away from the rolling echo. In cases where there is no echo a similar effect may be obtained by using a slow-burning squib type of banger which will give the sound of a shot at spaced intervals. By setting up a series of bangs at places where the birds might be expected to withdraw, they may frequently be moved successfully over the waiting guns.

Weather

The roughshooter should always consider the weather and the wind, or lack of it, when pigeon shooting. In icy conditions, with snow on the ground, pigeons will frequently flight in on any exposed green food with insatiable appetite, intent on cramming their crops during the short hours of daylight. They may then sometimes be shot without decoys and even with little or no attempt at concealment on the shooter's part. They will come in regardless of their fate. They may still have to be shot to protect the crop, but in such circumstances not only are they barely worth shooting, they are usually uneatable and unsaleable when shot.

If there is a thick mist, decoying is fairly obviously out of the question. When there is little or no wind, flighting the birds in to roost is also less likely to be successful. The birds will be circling high above the wood and the sound of shots will be enough to send them out of danger. When it is raining heavily the birds will also be barely worth shooting, if they are flying at all. The ideal conditions are a reasonably strong wind and good visibility without a bright sun. Shooting into the sun is always a difficult business anyway and then siting decoys and hides the effect of the sun during the day should be borne in mind.

Flighting in to Water

In very hot weather pigeons may sometimes be decoyed and shot in otherwise unsuitable conditions while coming in to water. A conveniently sited pond, or even a field trough, may sometimes provide a regular stream of birds coming to slake their thirst. In suitable conditions it is sometimes possible to make quite a useful bag by siting a hide within shot of such a source of water and simply taking the birds as they come. A single lofted decoy may encourage inquisitive passing birds in such circumstances to come in close enough for a shot. In all forms of flighting passage birds a lofted decoy is always worthwhile.

Learning to Predict Movements

The roughshooter who wants to be a successful pigeon shooter should always be prepared to experiment. He should also always keep his eyes open and watch the birds themselves. If he examines the crops of the birds he shoots he will usually learn something about their feeding habits. If he watches their reactions to the weather and to the feed available throughout the various seasons of the year he will in time be able to predict their movements and reactions with considerable accuracy. Thereafter his sport will be redoubled and he will always find some interesting and enjoyable shooting to be had on the roughshoot at various levels even during the close season.

8

Ground Game on the Roughshoot

THE RABBIT: *Oryctolagus cuniculus cuniculus*

The Name and the Public Image

The Latin name for the rabbit, *Oryctolagus cuniculus cuniculus*, has a fine ringing sound to it. It is from the Latin *cuniculus* that the old name for the rabbit for 'coney' originated. The name rabbit is, oddly enough, derived from a Walloon word 'rabbett' meaning a young rabbit. Since the days of Beatrix Potter and the Flopsy Bunnies the town dweller has probably seen rabbits as symbolising the peacefulness and tranquillity of country life. The more dangerous world of *Watership Down* may have changed the image slightly but not a great deal. However, if town dwellers knew the full background to the spread of the disease myxomatosis and realised the implications of it for the human race they might have very different thoughts on seeing rabbits.

The Background to Myxomatosis

There is an extremely frightening lesson for everyone in the deliberate wilful spreading of this disease. The very casualness with which a major epidemic affecting the livelihood of thousands of people was started by one man unaware of the far-reaching consequences of his actions is terrifying. The fact that an industry worth £140 millions could be ruined never came within his calculations. He was only concerned with his own affairs. That one man can cause the deaths of millions of animals without even realising what he was doing is horrific by any standards.

The disease itself was first reported in 1898 in South America, but it was not until 1927 that the idea of spreading it deliberately to 'control' rabbits was suggested. Then in 1936 the first experiments in this direction took place in Australia, continuing until 1943 and proving only partially successful. It was only after the war in 1951 and 1952 that a high mortality rate was achieved in Southern Australia.

The French Connection

In June 1952 a retired French doctor, a M. Armand Delille, who had inherited a small rabbit-infested estate in the country near Paris, innoculated two rabbits with the myxoma virus which he had obtained from a friend in a laboratory in Switzerland. Without apparently consulting his neighbours, or giving any local warnings, he released the two on his ground. It then spread so rapidly that by early 1953 it had appeared in the south of France despite strenuous efforts by the French government to contain it. In the same year it reached Britain and by 1954 was beginning to spread throughout the country, finally putting the entire rabbit trapping and fur and felt making industry out of business to the premature cheers of a small agricultural lobby.

The Effects

The amazing feature of the whole affair is that, although exhaustive tests had been performed in the laboratories, no one knew whether or not the disease might mutate and attack humans, or other animals. There is indeed no certainty even now that this might not happen. No one is in a position to say positively that it might not do so. To open such a Pandora's box on the world was irresponsible in the extreme and in practice the whole concept has proved both dangerous and futile. The rabbit has survived and any outbreaks of myxomatosis today are likely to be brief and to kill only a few of the local populations, acting on the rest more as a form of inoculation against future infection. Thus with each outbreak the resistance against the disease appears to grow stronger.

Symptoms

The disease itself is a disgusting one to watch, although scientific theoreticians in their laboratories maintain the rabbit feels no pain. The clinical description is that it has an incubation period of from five to six days prior to a watery discharge from the eyes. This thickens to pus within a day or so and the eyelids swell and redden, sticking together and causing blindness. Further similar swellings to the base of the nose and ears, under the chin, around the anus and genitals, as well as possibly on the body and feet may be visible and ensure that the animal can barely breathe, hear or perform its normal bodily functions. Death usually occurs from eleven to eighteen days after infection and the morality rate in the laboratory is 99.5 per cent. It is not a pleasant disease to spread cold-bloodedly and since that elusive 0.5 per cent still survives even in the laboratory and rather more so in the wild the disease does not even do what it was intended to do, namely exterminate the rabbit entirely.

The Past and Present

There was a time before myxomatosis was deliberately spread throughout Europe in the 1950s when rabbits were the mainstay of any roughshoot throughout the country, providing occasional shooting during otherwise dull moments and making up the bulk of the bag at the end of the day. Now the rabbit is staging a steady return and today in many areas they are almost as plentiful as they once were. This may not be to everyone's liking, but for the roughshooter it is a very desirable state of affairs. Once again he can rely on rabbits to make an interesting bag on an otherwise undistinguished shoot. It has indeed reached the stage in many areas where it is advisable to check a shooting lease carefully. The shooting tenant may be held liable for damage caused by rabbits and where a crop is severely damaged this liability may be for substantial sums running into thousands of pounds.

Origins

Although it might well be thought otherwise, the rabbit is not indigenous to this country. It was almost certainly introduced by the Normans, since there is no note of rabbit warrens in the Domesday Book, that great national survey which was printed in 1086.

Subsequently, during the Middle Ages the rabbit was deliberately bred in large artificial warrens and thus gradually populated the countryside. With the internecine warfare between Roundheads and Royalists of the Cromwellian Revolution in the 1630s no doubt warrens were sacked and pillaged wholesale by warring troops of both sides and rabbits allowed to escape throughout the countryside.

In Scotland

Strangely enough rabbits were scarcely known in Scotland even as late as 1800, although today they are as common in many parts of Scotland as anywhere else in Britain. The explanation is that they were deliberately introduced and encouraged, as much for their sporting value as for their meat or their fur. There are parts of Scotland where the rabbit is the only beast that could survive and where they are still flourishing. The reason for the amazing spread of the rabbit is similar to that of the wood pigeon, which was equally unknown in Scotland in the early 1800s. The development of sporting estates in Scotland in the 1840s during the Balmoralisation of the Highlands, followed by the decline of agriculture and at the same time the development of the cheap mass-produced breech-loading shotgun resulting in an immediate growth in the popularity of shooting all combined to encourage the spread of any bird or beast easily encouraged to breed and provide cheap meat and interesting sport.

Habits and Habitat

Rabbits are polygamous, indeed quite promiscuous in their matings. Watching them for any length of time it is usually possible to observe a mating as a buck quite casually mounts a doe. On one occasion I watched three rabbits nose to tail in Indian file, rather in the manner of hares in March, cross a road from a plantation and then run round in a circle in the grass field on the other side for some minutes. Finally they stopped and it soon transpired they were two bucks following a doe in season, for one of the bucks mounted her while the other crouched watching. They then went round in another circle and the second buck took his turn mounting the doe. This went on for around a quarter of an hour until I interrupted the proceedings by walking to the hedge in full view. One buck then went off to some cover and the other two clapped down in the grass making themselves inconspicuous in the manner of almost all wild creatures when aware of danger.

Double Oestrus

In addition to promiscuous matings, or perhaps as a result, second fertilisations, or double oestrus, are common amongst both rabbits and hares. Their gestation period is only six weeks and the young rabbits are born without fur and blind, but developing fur and reaching the stage of looking after themselves within about three weeks. Soon after this their mother may desert them, or conceivably have a second litter. With a second birth soon after the first, the two litters may perhaps be raised as one.

The Stop

Not long before it kindles, i.e. gives birth, a female rabbit will usually dig a short blind tunnel, or 'stop'. Inside a burrow this may consist of a side passage, off the main burrow. In very crowded burrows the doe may go outside to dig this stop, sensing danger to her young from old bucks in the warren who may find the young and kill them, as sometimes happens. A stop in the open, of course, is also subject to predation by anything from hunting stoats or weasels to dogs and cats. When the stop has been dug the female then lines it with dried grass and wool from her coat and is ready to kindle.

Colours

Colour mutations are quite common in otherwise ordinary litters. I have seen white, black and piebald, as well as bright yellow and distinctly orange rabbits, all on the same ground, and quite clearly coming from various litters with otherwise perfectly normal litter brothers and sisters. Such mutations are easily identified and in a large warren may be watched with interest. Of the various mutations the lemon yellow is probably the rarest, although the bright orange, which may be seen on the neck hairs of many rabbits, I have only encountered in a few isolated areas and it may have something to do with the sandy soil and its constituents. The black, the white, and the black and white, are common enough in many places.

Size and Weight

The size of rabbits may vary enormously depending almost entirely on the feeding available. I have frequently encountered full grown rabbits not much larger than half the average size at the top of a hill which held large numbers of rabbits and in fact amounted to a large warren. The ones at the top simply lacked the feeding of those near the bottom and never had a chance to grow beyond what amounted to half the normal size of those on the lusher feeding beneath them. The normal weight of a fully grown rabbit is between 2–3 lbs. Females, especially in doe, will often weigh much more and, along with full grown and particularly well fed bucks, may even go up to 5 lbs, but this is quite exceptional.

Shooting and Safety

Whatever its size and location, however, the rabbit should provide sporting opportunities for the roughshooter. The rabbit bouncing between tufts of grass in a meadow and moving at speed can provide a testing shot for any gun, but it is always important to have a care when rabbit shooting. It is not only necessary to watch out for dogs hunting in front, but for the proximity of any other guns.

A rabbit running between two guns may cause an excitable novice to take a dangerous shot. Even at an angle of forty-five degrees a shot at ground game may result in a ricochet from stony ground and cause a pellet to hit a neighbouring gun. It only requires one such pellet in the eye for irreparable harm to be done. Always take care when shooting ground game of any kind. This applies especially when two roughshooters are walking up each side of a hedge, or plantation strip, or when two guns are waiting for rabbits to bolt from holes. Always allow the rabbits to get well clear before taking a shot. **Never** shoot when you cannot see exactly where the shot will go.

Flying Rabbits

Perhaps one of the most satisfactory shots that can be taken at rabbits is when they are running along the face of a hill above the gun, or when they are bolting at full speed up a steep slope. Then when cleanly shot they will frequently leap in the air to roll downwards and land almost in the jaws of the dog hunting below or at the feet of the gun himself. Such 'flying' rabbits can provide exceptional sport at times.

Snap Shots

The snap shot at rabbits on the edge of a hole as they are so often encountered when coming over a small rise can also be a testing shot. Even when killed outright they may still summon up enough nervous reflexes to jerk their way down the hole beyond the reach of the questing dog, or even the arm of the roughshooter. The only solution then may be to dig them out, but it is seldom the roughshooter will have a spade handy unless he is ferreting. Such rabbits may often thus be lost to the bag.

Ferreting

Ferreting is a sport in itself and ferrets, both hobs and jills as they are termed, are as individual and interesting beasts to keep as dogs. Like dogs they should be kept clean and properly fed and housed in a warm hutch with their bedding changed frequently. They should be handled, fed by hand regularly and called to the whistle so that they are accustomed to their handler and do not bite him. Biting and fierceness in a ferret are usually a sign that it has been handled incorrectly. Given plenty of attention they will then soon learn what is required of them when introduced to the rabbit burrow.

Whether the roughshooter uses purse nets, or a .410, or .410 adaptors in his 12 bore, he should have good sport with a ferret as the rabbits bolt in turn. The time of year, the weather and the approach are all important. It is absurd ferreting in high summer when the ferret is likely to get into a stop and gorge itself on young rabbits, taking its fill and lying up until moved by hunger to come to the surface. Then too the cover is so high that bolting rabbits may sneak unseen from overgrown holes and escape. The ideal time for ferreting is from November onwards to February or March, when the growth is short and the rabbits are not likely to be breeding. It is, of course, theoretically possible to work the ferrets at any time of year, but it should be regarded as generally a sport to practise towards the end of the shooting season and soon after it is over.

Lie-ups

Micro-chip technology has produced a tiny bug incorporated into a nylon ferret harness which is easily located with a detector from above ground. This is now an accepted part of the ferreting scene. It is thus possible to work out exactly where the ferret is laid-up when it fails to surface. It is thus comparatively easy to dig down from above ground directly to the ferret, instead of the old painful method of following a line-ferret, sent down with a nylon cord on a harness to locate the missing beast, or digging out the hole which often meant moving half a hillside. In some cases, however, it may still be necessary to leave a travelling box beside the hole along with some feed and trust that in the morning the ferret will be waiting. Like hunting and losing a hound, ferreting can have its anxious moments, as well as provide some fascinating sport.

Snaring

Snaring rabbits is an old country pastime and one which can be quite challenging. Tim Sedgwick, the editor of *The Shooting Times* after the Second World War, used to set a line of snares in the hedge as he went to catch his morning commuter train to London and then duly lifted his supper on his way back in the evening. If they are not inspected early enough each morning, however, a fox will probably have relieved you of the rabbits caught, leaving only the head behind or perhaps removing the snare as well.

'A hand's breadth high for a rabbit and half a hand more for a hare' runs the old country saw, which is accurate enough depending on the size of the hand. I myself was taught to snare in the Highlands at the age of four by a reprobate of fully six months my senior. He used to catch on average half a dozen rabbits a day, most of them in home-made snares of string. Even at that tender age there was little he did not know about the sport.

Not everyone can be fortunate in having such a mentor, but the roughshooter should find that a few well placed snares can provide him with rabbits in those tricky patches on the edge of woods with crops growing alongside where there are numerous rabbits and traces of runs, but no shot is possible until the crops are harvested. This can be an interesting pastime and combined with a trap round should help to broaden the roughshooter's experience. If the snares become the target for predators – foxes, mink, stoats, or crows – then that in itself should tell the roughshooter that he is not doing his job fully. Fox snares, tunnel traps or other means may be required to redress the balance.

On the Roughshoot

Wherever the roughshoot may be there are likely to be traces of a few rabbits on it somewhere. One way or another they should provide some sport. It is up to the roughshooter to decide how to make the best of it, whether by shooting, snaring or ferreting, or possibly all three. Of course not all such rabbits may be living in burrows beneath ground. In many areas there are what used to be termed scrub rabbits lying out above ground and living in the open in a scrape, much after the manner of hares lying in a form.

Scrub Rabbits

Scrub rabbits are most likely to be encountered in low-lying marshy areas, where to dig a hole would merely be to find it filling with water, but they may also be encountered almost anywhere including very rocky ground where digging holes is difficult. Such rabbits are less inclined to be found infested with rabbit fleas, which pass the myxoma virus, hence many of these rabbits living above ground escaped the infection. Such rabbits seem to cover much larger territories than rabbits living below ground and their behaviour in many ways is more akin to hares.

Where there is an abundance of such scrub rabbits living in the open, very good sport may be had with a dog, either pointing them, or bustling them out of cover. Similar sport can be had with rabbits in burrows if the holes are blocked while the rabbits are out feeding. A little paper soaked in paraffin, or similar smelly substance thrust down the holes will suffice to keep the rabbits on the surface and the following day they may be hunted up with dogs in the same way as scrub rabbits. This can be a surprisingly effective way of ensuring a good bag of rabbits.

THE BROWN HARE: *Lepus Europeus*

The common brown hare in the U.K. is known as *Lepus Europeus* and at one time was found nearly everywhere. Unfortunately, with the regular use of toxic sprays on most growing crops the brown hare appears to be diminishing steadily in numbers just as the rabbit is returning in full force. In addition to modern farming methods, almost all of which seem weighted against them, hares also suffer a great many casualties on the roads. It is very sad that a creature once so plentiful should now be far less common than of old in many areas of the country. It appears to be becoming less and less common every year in heavily populated parts of the country. It can, however, still be found in something like reasonable numbers in some areas. It is, as the name implies, mainly brown in colouring with black tips to the long ears. Size may vary considerably, largely dependent on the feeding available, but colouring remains much the same throughout the country. Weight may vary from around 6 lbs for an adult hare to as much as 12 lbs in some areas. One of the first I ever weighed, since it was in the descriptive Irish phrase 'as big as a donkey', weighed in at over 13 lbs, which is close to the British record of $13\frac{1}{4}$ lbs. The average is probably about 8 lbs.

Habits and Habitat

The accepted breeding season for hares in the U.K. is from February to August and they may not be sold during this period. On the other hand, hares will certainly breed several times a year and much must depend on the severity of the winter and the general weather conditions. Thus hares may breed three or four times a year and may rear young, known as leverets, at any time, even if principally during the spring.

During March especially, mating fever is likely to grip the hares and cause them to lose their normal timidity. They will run in circles in grass or stubble fields and may even form hare parliaments when as many as fifteen or more may form a circle and play follow my leader in circles and figures of eight. At one time such sights were common enough in many parts of the country but with the overall decrease in hares they are now a rarity. In the throes of mating frenzy hares will stand and box each other, or run in circles, close to and completely ignoring the presence of humans, or even dogs, of whom they would normally be afraid.

The Leverets

The young leverets, only about a couple of inches long at birth, are born fully furred and as many as four or five may be born at one time. The phenomenon of double oestrus, as with rabbits, may also arise in hares, owing to the promiscuity of their matings. The young are removed from the form in which they are born shortly after birth and carried by their mother to separate points where each is hidden and the mother then feeds them in turn.

Background

The hare has for long been regarded by country people as having a touch of mystery about it. One of the earliest records of them is by William Twici, huntsman to Edward III, in his *L'Art de Venerie*, in which he wrote of the hare: 'She is the most marvellous beast . . . at one time it is male and at another female.' For a great part of the Middle Ages right up to the 18th century the hare was associated in credulous country minds with witchcraft and it is true that hermaphrodite hares are not all that uncommon.

Concealment

The ability of the hare to conceal itself in a seemingly impossible patch of tiny cover has, however, to be seen to be believed. The hare's habit of running at full speed up to another hare lying in its form, but unseen by the pursuer, and butting on the sitting hare which promptly vacates its form and sets off at speed, thus allowing the pursuing dog to continue on its way is also remarkable to watch. In over forty years of watching, shooting and hunting hares, I have only seen this at close quarters twice and it is very understandable why a dog pursuing at speed would overlook the hare in its form and continue after the fresh hare running in front.

Going to Ground

It should be added that although brown hares are not supposed to go to ground I have known this happen. I once watched a young dog course a hare round a walled garden when suddenly it appeared at a loss as the hare had disappeared. On investigation I found a damaged manhole cover over a drain with a hole in one corner. I lifted it and could hear a steady panting from the darkness below. The hare had obviously decided that this was a game it did not wish to play and had headed for cover. Satisfied at having solved the mystery I left it undisturbed still panting like a steam engine.

THE BLUE HARE: *Lepus Timidus*

The blue mountain hare, or *Lepus Timidus*, does very readily take to cover and may sometimes be found in short burrows, although it also makes scrapes, or forms, like the brown hare. There are to be precise two species of blue mountain hare, *Lepus Timidus Scoticus* and *Lepus Timidus Hibernicus*, the latter found in Ireland. The difference appears to be that only the Scottish hare turns completely white in colour in winter and the Irish hare is likely to weigh a little more as well as moving in company with others of its kind.

Size and Weight

The blue hare is lighter boned than the brown hare and weighs in general less, being on average about 6–7 lbs. They can however be as much as 8 or 9 lbs depending as ever on the feeding available. The meat of the blue hare is usually regarded as inferior to that of the brown hare, but I am inclined to think this is largely a matter of the feeding available and the cooking. I have found blue hares on occasions extremely good eating and certainly as good, if not better than some brown hares.

The Effects of Feeding

There certainly can be no doubt that rabbits and indeed all ground game vary extremely in size and weight, as well as flavour, dependent on the feeding. For instance in one area I know where wild garlic abounds the rabbits' flesh actually smells very strongly of garlic. So much is this the case that a rabbit shot amongst this wild garlic will be passed over by dogs simply because it does not smell of rabbit but of garlic. While being gutted and skinned the smell of garlic in these beasts is very noticeable. Left in the deep freeze the smell of garlic is almost overpowering and when cooked the flavour is still very strong. This is but one example, if an unusual one, of the noticeable effects of feeding on ground game, but what affects rabbits must also affect hares in much the same way.

Clean Shooting

One final word on the subject of shooting ground game. It is always important to swing right through and take both rabbits and hares in the head, killing them cleanly, so that if well executed they will cartwheel over stone-dead. With hares particularly, because of their larger size it is easy for inexperienced shots to hit them behind and merely wound them. It is imperative to swing right through and kill them cleanly. If seen to flinch but run on, a hare is probably hit in the lungs and may well be picked up stone-dead sometimes several hundred yards further on. A good dog should be set on the line to fetch it.

Walking up behind pointing dogs on the moor.

Left: A successful retrieve of a grouse. *Right:* A successful
retrieve of a rabbit.

The ferret emerging from the rabbit hole after successfully
bolting the rabbit into the purse net.

Left: Home-made oil drum feed hopper. *Right:* Filling a
home-made oil drum feed hopper.

Left: Using a ditch to wait for passage pigeons.
Above: Using a drainage hole for passage pigeons.
Below: Flighting pigeons on the edge of a wood.

Loading the gun: safe (*right hand gun*); unsafe (*left hand gun*).

Left: Lofting decoy on tree-top platform.

Left: Spying for deer. *Right:* Rifle at the ready with arm through sling.

Left: Aiming at the stand with arm through sling giving support. *Right:* Sitting with rifle supported on knees and arm through sling.

Left: Using a stick and kneeling, with arm through sling. *Right:* Prone position with arm through sling.

Left: Tunnel trap sticked and covered with turf beside rearing pen.

Above: Tunnel trap with covering of turf removed.

Above: Baiting a cage trap for mink at the water's edge.

Right: A fox snare set in a run.

Finding the deer with a dog.

A comfortable method of carrying deer a long way but inclined to be messy.

9

Deer and the Rifle on the Roughshoot

The Background

It is largely the effect of the British firearms laws that we tend to think of roughshooting as restricted to small game shot with the shotgun, rather than including all the beasts that may be found on the roughshoot, and the use of a rifle. To some extent also it is a hangover from the rigidly compartmented minds of the Victorian English who differentiated between hunting and different forms of shooting. Hunting to them meant following a pack of hounds and shooting meant going out with a shotgun, while deer stalking meant going out with a rifle after deer.

The Elizabethan Englishman regarded hunting as going out after a quarry, whether with dogs alone or with dogs and a gun. This is the definition of hunting around most of the rest of the world today. It is the definition I prefer, for there is no doubt that a man going out with dogs on a roughshoot is hunting, just as a man going out with a rifle after deer, whether he has a dog or not is also hunting. Essentially, when a man is in search of a quarry he is hunting. Thus I see no reason for excluding deer from the roughshoot. To my mind if they are present they may be stalked, or hunted, and as the law of the land rightly only allows them to be killed with a rifle, then so be it. It is important, however, that they should be included in the shooting lease, otherwise the deer stalking may be let separately.

The average roughshoot is unlikely to have more than one or, at the most, two varieties of deer on it, but in fact it is surprising how few roughshooters know anything about deer at all. Indeed it is amazing how many people never see deer and are even unaware that they are to be found on their ground. Unless they happen to come across them by accident or see them break away in the middle of a drive with white tails bobbing over a field they may well be surprised to learn there are deer on their shoot.

Distribution

The most widely distributed deer in the U.K. is probably the roe, with the fallow and red next most prevalent. Less common, if widely scattered in small areas, is the Japanese Sika deer. Spreading rapidly in many areas today is the small muntjac, or barking deer, and least common of all is the Chinese water deer, which is restricted to a comparatively small area. Apart from the Chinese water deer all are distinguished by the fact that the males grow antlers while the females, with some very rare exceptions, do not.

The Antlers

Most male deer, with the exception of muntjac, cast their antlers at a set time of the year and start almost immediately growing a fresh set. These grow from the pedicle, small knobs on either side of the skull, on which is formed the coronet, or burr, forming the base of the antlers. When there is a soft hairy skin covering the growing antlers this is known as being 'in velvet'. When the antlers are full grown the soft horn underneath the velvet hardens and the blood supply is cut off. The velvet then begins to irritate and is rubbed off against trees and bushes in a process known as fraying. Once the velvet has been removed the antlers are said to be clean.

Digestion

All deer are ruminants, with four chambers in the stomach. They cut their food against a hard pad of flesh in the upper jaw with the sharp incisor teeth in the lower jaw and grind their food with their cheek teeth. The food is stored in the first compartment of the stomach, or rumen. It is regurgitated at leisure while resting in cover later when a cheekful, the cud, is chewed slowly before being swallowed and beginning the process of digestion in a second compartment of the stomach, the reticulum. The cheek is then refilled from the rumen and the ruminating process is continued until the food is fully digested.

Feeding

Deer eat mostly at dawn or dusk, but when there is a full moon they may continue to eat through much of the night. Where they are not disturbed during the day, however, they will continue to eat, although spending lengthy periods ruminating. They are grazers, eating almost any kind of herbage, as well as browsers, stripping the branches of bushes and trees and eating the leaves and bark. Their choice of food is extremely varied, depending to some extent on their environment but extending from root and cereal crops to grass, fungi, mosses, brackens, ferns, heather, almost any berries, chestnuts, beech mast and acorns. It is the damage they do to trees and bushes by stripping bark from them or damaging them by fraying with their antlers as well as trampling corn or young hay that is probably most serious.

Senses

They have large eyes and are quick to notice movement, although they often appear to find it hard to distinguish what they see, so that if a stalker freezes in position he is often apparently mistaken for a boulder or part of a tree. They also tend not to look upwards, unlike ground game or gamebirds, which have one eye constantly alert for hawks or danger from above. The deer's ears, however, are constantly moving and they will pick up strange sounds at a considerable distance. They also have fine powers of scent and can pick up the scent of humans at remarkable distances.

Movements

When feeding in the open deer may be seen to be continually raising their heads and looking round, scenting the wind and using their ears to alert them to the approach of danger. In woodland they will rely on hearing and scent more than sight and on absolute immobility, freezing into the shadows, rather than instant flight. They may also creep round in cover keeping a bush or other protection between them and any possible danger. At the same time they are curious creatures and this can sometimes be their undoing since a deer may well bound off in flight at the first hint of danger, then halt after some twenty or thirty yards and peer back motionless to try to identify what it was that startled it. This may well provide a perfect opportunity for the stalker to take a successful shot.

RED DEER: *Cervus elaphus*

The differences between the various kinds of deer are considerable. The largest is the red deer, *Cervus elaphus*, one of the two deer indigenous to the U.K. The males and females are known as stags and hinds and the young as calves. The stag sheds his antlers each spring and they are re-grown by late summer. The antler growth is entirely predictable apart from cases of injury. At two years the male calf grows a small knob on each side of his head and is known as a knobber. By six years he is near full grown and will have light antlers of 7 or 8 points. By eight years he is in his prime and from then to thirteen or fourteen years may grow a full head of 12 points which is termed a royal. Thereafter he will be regarded as an old stag going back and will lose points and should be culled. Those stags which never grow antlers are known as hummels; they may be very large beasts and should be culled whenever seen. Another which should always be shot whenever possible is the stag with just 4, or worse still, only 2 points, the most lethal of heads, liable to kill stags with much better heads. Switch heads, as they are known, should always be shot.

The red deer's coat is normally a short reddish-brown with thick grey undercoat, but there are many colour variations, although melanistic black, or white, are very uncommon. The stags have a distinctive ridge of coarse hair along the spine and neck which during the rut, or mating season, becomes a mane. They will grow up to 40–45 inches (101–114 cm) at the shoulder and on the hill weigh from 14 to 16 stone (88–102 kg) but lowland stags may weigh almost twice as much. The hind is more lightly built, between 38–42 inches (96–104 cm) at the shoulder and weighing from around 8–11 stone (50–70 kg). They are unlikely to live beyond fifteen. Calves are born around May or June. The rut begins around mid-September and continues until the end of October. This is when the stags fight and challenge each other giving an impressive roaring sound, the victorious stags collecting a harem of females. They are gregarious but the stags live away from the hinds except during the rut. After the rut a herd of hinds with calves and yearlings of from ten upwards to fifty or more will be led by an old hind.

The red deer is commonest in the Highlands but is found in

Cumbria and in the West Country as well as in the New Forest and Thetford Chase. Otherwise it is mainly restricted to deer parks scattered around the country. Like a horse it can walk, trot, canter and gallop. Its most characteristic pace is a steady trot with head held erect, but it can cover considerable distances at a gallop and can jump extremely well. There will not be many roughshoots where red deer are likely to be encountered, but they have been known to wander considerable distances so that a stray red deer may be met with quite unexpectedly.

FALLOW DEER: *Dama dama*

Probably more common on the roughshoot will be feral fallow deer, or *Dama dama*, the best known of British deer. The male is termed a buck and the female a doe, while the young are fawns. The buck sheds his antlers in April or May and they are usually out of velvet by September. Unlike the other deer in Britain the antlers are palmated, or flattened towards the outer tips. There is only a minimal difference in size between bucks and does. When full grown the buck stands about 32–36 inches (81–96 cm) at the shoulder, does from 32–34 inches (81–86 cms), while the average weight of the bucks is from 9–10 stone (57–63 kg) and does from 7–8 stone (44–50 kg).

The fallow deer were probably originally introduced to the British Isles by the Normans and have been the favourite park deer ever since. With the effects of the Civil War in the 1630s they naturally spread into the wild in considerable numbers as park walls were knocked down and estates pillaged by rival troops. Since then there have in addition been numerous escapes from parks which have increased their numbers around the country, even up to and including the last war. It is scarcely surprising therefore that the colours of coat are very variable with at least seven recognised varieties, which makes it plain enough why it is often difficult to recognise a fallow deer without antlers. The fallow buck, however, has a prominent brush, or tail, around 6 inches (15 cm) long.

Perhaps the best way to tell fallow deer when without their antlers is by their reactions and gait when startled. If they are much harried they will move off at a fast gallop at the first sign of danger, but if normally undisturbed, their first reaction to an alarm is uncertainty. They may even approach with ears cocked and neck upright taking several uncertain steps with stiff legs. They then bound off with stiff legs in a manner peculiar to fallow deer known as 'pronking', but even then they will probably stop near to cover and look back, allowing the stalker time for a shot. The doe will sometimes bark when alarmed and they are good jumpers.

Like both red and sika deer they are gregarious. Like red deer, the bucks form groups for much of the year, although the old bucks go off alone. The does and young form separate herds and the two only combine at the rut. Fawns are usually born around mid-May and twins are very rare. At the time of the rut the buck forms a rutting stand and defends his territory, but unlike the red deer does not often have to herd his does, which gather round him. He gives tongue with a belching roar at intervals and smells extremely rank.

JAPANESE SIKA: *Cervus nippon*

The Japanese Sika, *Cervus nippon*, is about the same size as the fallow deer, the stags standing 32–34 inches (81–86 cm) and weighing around 8–10 stone (50–63 kg) while the hind stands 30–32 inches (76–81 cm) and weighs about 5–7 stone (34–44 kg). The young, as with red deer, are known as calves. Their body colour is reddish-brown with yellowish spots showing faintly on the flanks in summer. In winter the coat is darker brown above and grey below. The head is usually noticeably paler and greyer and there is an obvious U-shaped mark above the eyes. The caudal patch is noticeably white and lined with black, flaring when frightened and very prominent in full flight. The stags cover the ground at a heavy gallop when alarmed, and at a walk move rather furtively.

It is possible that one herd of Sika may be a slightly different variety from another as their behaviour appears to vary from area to area, ranging between the behaviour of red deer and that of fallow. They generally have harems and in some places appear to be territorial and in others not. The stag has a very distinctive whistling call which is quite different from any other deer and is unmistakable. The normal full grown head of af mature sika stag is only 8 points, although with slight palmation of the main beam it may become 10, or even 11 points.

ROE DEER: *Capreolus capreolus*

Roe deer, *Capreolus capreolus*, along with the red deer the only indigenous deer, is quite different in behaviour to the others so far mentioned. The buck sheds his antlers around mid-October and they are usually re-grown and clear of velvet by March. The kids are born in May to June and by November the kid has buttons formed on the pedicles. The first antlers are grown as bony spikes and the youngster may be termed a spiker. The full head of a mature buck may have 6 points and be around 8 inches (20 cm) long, but seldom more than 10 inches (25 cm). Up to around the age of six or seven the antlers should improve each year, growing rougher and thicker with small growths known as pearling and ridged channels known as gutters. There are normally 3 points known as the brow, top and rear points. The average size of buck and doe is the same, about 25–30 inches (63–76 cms) at the shoulder and about 44 inches (112 cm) from muzzle to rump, weighing around 35–65 lbs (20–29 kg) full grown. As ever, much must depend on the quantity and quality of the feeding available.

In summer the coat is a bright reddish-brown with a pale underbelly. Then the caudal disc beneath the rump has a distinctive white colouring and is known as the target. They also have a white patch under the chin and in front of the notably dark muzzle. With their long ears and alert eyes they have an expression of curiosity and interest. There are variations in colour with some roe noticeably darker than others and some with a dark streak down the centre of the spine.

Like most deer they are elderly at ten and how old they may live is hard to say, but it is doubtful if it is over fourteen years. In youth they have an obviously slender neck and sloping rump. In middle age they have a well filled body and neck and in old age carry the neck almost level with the body and the gait becomes stiffer.

They are not often seen to trot, preferring to walk daintily or else bound along at a gentle canter, sometimes stopping to look back at what has alarmed them. They may also be seen creeping along in a hunched posture to avoid being seen. Like most deer they can jump exceedingly well. They can swim well and have been seen swimming considerable stretches of water.

Although not strictly monogamous the roe are frequently seen together in small family groups of buck, doe, yearling and kids. They do not usually form herds, although groups of twenty or so may sometimes be seen feeding together during the winter months. In the spring a mature buck will drive off the younger bucks in the family group to find their own territory and will mark out an area of about ten acres (4 ha) or thereabouts in woodland, or even more, as much as half a mile (1 km) in open upland ground. He will mark his territory by fraying and anointing chosen trees with the scent glands in his forehead and inner corners of the eye. Scrapes may also be made in the ground, impregnated with urine as scenting markers.

The buck will at times be heard barking a challenge. Both buck and doe will occasionally bark loudly to announce their presence, or in alarm. The meaning of the barks is not always plain and can apparently sometimes express disgust at an intrusion rather than alarm at the presence of danger.

Twin kids are normal and triplets are not uncommon, although single births are also possible. The kids are reddish-brown with creamy spots on the flanks which they soon lose. They are hidden in separate cover in bracken, or similar soft beds. In late May and through June the doe often plays with the kids, chasing them and teaching them to leap and jump. This makes a most attractive sight but as it usually takes place in woodland, or in thick cover, is not often seen.

The rut takes place in July to August and the preliminaries may take weeks, although the doe is only in season for around four days. The buck shows attention to the doe, following her closely. The doe will run in rings and figures of eight with the buck's nose pressing on her posterior. During this period the buck completely loses his usual caution and may be seen frequently in daylight hours. Though naturally a forest dweller they are also found in the uplands; they are widely distributed through Scotland and are extending their range in the south annually, although none are to be found in Wales.

THE MUNTJAC: *Muntiacus muntjak*

The Indian Muntjac, *Muntiacus muntjak*, is a comparative newcomer, having escaped from Woburn Park in Bedfordshire since the last war. The male is known as a buck and the female as doe while the young are fawns. There may be two varieties, the Indian and the Reevse, also hybrids of the two, present in the wild. The bucks may vary in size from 17–23 inches (43–58.5 cm) with the does around 3 inches (7.5 cm) less. The average buck weighs around 25–30 lbs (11–13 kg) with the doe about 2–5 lbs (1–2 kg) lighter.

The body is a deep chestnut-red in colour with a darker back and paler belly. They have a 6 inch (15 cm) tail which is raised when running away and shows a distinctive white underside. Most distinctive feature of all, however, in the bucks are the short $2\frac{1}{2}$–3 inch (6–7.5 cm) antlers which grow from long skin-covered pedicles extending down the forehead, giving the deer the name of rib face. The bucks also have small tusks nearly $1\frac{1}{2}$ inches (4 cm) long. As well as the distinctive ribbed face they also have very blunt muzzles which gives them a noticeably Roman-nosed look. They are fast movers, covering the ground at a run with a hunched back and with the head held low, which is not attractive, but does not detract from their speed, nor their ability to jump, despite their short legs.

They are sometimes also called the barking deer and will give a single bark at about five second intervals for up to three quarters of an hour. They will sometimes bark together in chorus. They are also different in that there is no set season for the rut and does may give birth at any time of year, but usually produce a single fawn at eight month intervals.

CHINESE WATER DEER

The only other deer it is possible the roughshooter may encounter in this country is the Chinese water deer. The males are known as bucks the females does and the young fawns. They are much the same height as the Muntjac and stand slightly higher behind, but they do not have antlers. The buck has prominent tusks up to $2\frac{3}{4}$ inches (7 cm) long which protrude well below the jawline and can cause a nasty wound. They are reddish–brown in summer and greyer in winter time.

Their territories are marked by scrapes, and their alarm cry is a repeated bark. They are fast movers and can jump well, but are inclined to squat down in the open after running a comparatively short distance. Twins and triplets are common and the young are sexually mature at six months. It is clear, however, that a great deal more is to be learned about this species.

Deer on the Roughshoot

The roughshooter who has deer on his ground will enjoy both watching and stalking them whether during the shooting season itself or outside it. The presence of deer on the ground adds a fresh dimension to the sport available. It also brings the roughshooter on to the ground at times when he might not otherwise normally be there. Arriving on the roughshoot before dawn at any time of the year will provide him with a new insight into the ways of other wildlife on it.

As well as watching the deer feeding in the first light of day, he will hear the cock-up of the pheasants coming down from their roosts to feed, he will hear the chissicking of partridges and see their first flights from their jugging points to feed. He will see the hare settling down in its form and gain many other fresh angles on the game on his shoot. In addition, he may see badgers rolling purposefully back to their earths and he may also have a chance occasionally of turning his rifle onto a fox heading back from a raid on a poultry yard or other depredation.

Watching the natural world of his roughshoot unfolding before his eyes with the first dawn light can be not only interesting, but immensely valuable. While stalking, whether in the open on the hillside, or in the woodland, or combining both by sitting in a high seat on the woodland edge, the roughshooter stalker will learn a great deal about the ways of the animals and birds on his ground. The roughshoot should always benefit from the presence of the roughshooter on it but he will also gain in many ways.

Initial Approach

As far as stalking is concerned, of course, the roughshooter's first concern is to find how many deer there are on his ground and of what kinds. Only when he has established the varieties, their numbers and movements should he begin to consider which ones might be usefully culled. This, it may be appreciated, is not likely to be accomplished in a matter of weeks. It may even take several months before he is clear in his own mind where the various beasts he has seen fit into the overall pattern. Only then should he consider using his rifle, although it is always well to have it handy since at any time it is possible a crippled, or obviously sick, beast may be seen which it is best to cull at once.

Injured deer

Sadly, the number of deer seriously injured by cars or crippled by modern high tension fencing is considerable. Very often the stalker will find the remains of a deer hung up on a fence by a hind leg, and signs that it has ended its life in agony scratching up the earth with its forelegs before dying finally of starvation. Almost as bad is the case where the leg has snapped below the hock and after some initial struggles the deer has managed to drag itself away on three legs, leaving a severed stump behind to tell the tale. Admittedly quite a few such deer recover well enough to lead almost normal lives, but these are the exception rather than the rule and normally they should be shot as soon as possible.

The Aim

The aim should be taken just below the withers behind the shoulder. There is the school of thought which advocates coming up the line of the foreleg and shooting behind the leg as soon as the brown of the body is seen in the sights. True this may well result in a heart or lung shot. In either case the deer may well run as much as a hundred yards or more before collapsing dead, and in thick cover this may mean a lengthy search and even the loss of the beast. If by chance the leg itself is hit the result is a lame beast which may run miles. Either way a dog may be required to find the deer.

If the scope is brought down from above and lined up just behind the shoulder for the shot the chances are that if the shot goes high the deer will be clean missed. If it goes low it will be a lung shot, or break the shoulder and cause the beast to fall immobilised, or else break the spinal column and kill the beast stone-dead. Admittedly the meat on the spinal column is good eating, but the top of the shoulder is not up to much. It is open to argument that this is a better way of taking aim than coming up from below, but of course much must depend on the circumstances of the shot itself.

Undesirable Shots

It is never advisable to take a shot at a beast lying down, although it may mean a lengthy wait for it to rise. A sharp whistle may result in it springing to its feet alert for danger when a shot may be taken. No shot should ever be taken through bushes, branches or grass, which may deflect the bullet and may mean a wounded beast. Nor should shots be taken at moving beasts unless they are already wounded and it is a question of trying to stop them getting away. Over long shots should never be taken and care should also be taken not to shoot when two beasts are side by side, since the bullet penetrating one deer may wound the other.

After the Shot

Once the trigger has been pulled and the shot taken the immediate reaction should be to reload, since a second shot may be required. It sometimes does happen that a deer is narrowly missed and hears the shot but is unsure where it came from, remaining still but alert. Alternatively, very often another deer previously unseen will appear on the scene and it may be desirable to shoot it also. It is also possible that the deer may only have been wounded and a second shot may be essential as soon as possible to make sure of it. On all counts it is important to reload at once as a matter of course. If reloading is fast enough, the sound of the bolt action is lost in the report of the shot and the wounded deer is less likely to locate the source of danger.

Reaction to the Shot

If the deer falls immediately it is always important to have a second bullet in the chamber in case it was only creased and knocked unconscious by, for instance, a bullet grazing the antlers. On the other hand, if it goes down slowly it may only be gut shot and after a few moments may recover and go off stiffly to run perhaps for miles before dying. If the deer leaps before setting off it is probably heart or lung shot and will not run far. The first thing the stalker should do is mark the spot and go to it at once, then search for any signs of blood or hair indicating a hit. Frothy blood will indicate a lung shot, thick red blood a body hit. It may then be possible to follow the blood trail and if the first few yards can be found the line will usually be fairly straight, allowing for the ground and the wounded beast taking the easiest route. In such circumstances it is usually best to allow half an hour for the beast to stiffen up and then fetch a dog to follow the trail.

The Binoculars

When it comes to stalking deer the roughshooter has to teach himself an entirely new approach. His binoculars are the important feature of his stalking and to a large extent they dictate his actions. Hung round his neck ready for instant use, there should be no metal pieces likely to catch in zips or buttons and make a noise. They should be light and handy as well as powerful. With them the stalker surveys each fresh piece of ground as it appears. It is a highly undesirable practice to use the rifle scope for viewing the ground as this could result in a dangerous accidental shot. Each time the scope is used in this way a loaded rifle is being pointed at random.

Still-hunting

When still-hunting in woodland, or low ground, the stalker should move extremely slowly, a good deal less than a mile an hour, dependent on the ground. Until he reaches the stalking ground his rifle should not be loaded. Only then may a round be slipped in and the safety catch left in place. With the rifle slung behind his left shoulder and the muzzle pointing downwards the stalker should be ready, if he has practised sufficiently, to slip it round to his right shoulder in one steady movement. If he curls his wrist and elbow through the sling he will then have a powerful leverage which will help to hold the rifle steady. He will not need to have his rifle at the ready until his binoculars reveal that the patch of red over there is the roe buck he has been looking for and expected to find on this ground, standing alertly facing sideways on. It should then be a simple matter slowly to raise the rifle into position making sure there is no sudden movement to attract the buck's attention.

In Open Ground

In the open it is advisable to start stalking from the high ground if possible. Once the deer are spotted from above it is then a question of circumventing them, by using the ground and the wind to get within range before they have moved. This may involve running fast in dead ground and slowly crawling over exposed ground. To get within range of the chosen beast is often a difficult task complicated by the presence of other deer, or other game such as grouse or pheasants, or even sheep. The stalker's aim in either case should be to take a clear shot from as close as possible to ensure a clean kill.

Range and Safety Margins

Anyone who boasts of taking shots at 200 yards and over is suspect. It is always desirable to take shots at no more than 150 yards and whenever possible a great deal less. That a rifle may have a lethal range of up to a mile or more does not mean that very long shots should be attempted. It does mean that the stalker has to have very different criteria on safety to the man armed with a shotgun. He must ensure that the background to all his shots is a safe one. He should never shoot at beasts on a skyline since a miss might mean a bullet travelling on in a parabola and killing or injuring people or stock. In the same way if there are stock beyond the deer, or worse still buildings in which people or stock may be found, it is essential not to shoot. Needless to say, with a rifle also, as with a shotgun, the same rules apply, particularly **never** shoot when you cannot see clearly where the shot may go.

Deer and The Roughshoot

The concept of keeping roughshooting and deer stalking apart is basically caused by the firearms laws of the country. It does not make sense on the ground. There is for example one shoot I know well which twenty years ago was a good pheasant shoot, having been well laid out before the war. The estate had been sold up at the end of the war and continued as a driven pheasant shoot for five or six years. Then one of the centre farms was sold so that it really in effect became two roughshoots just tenuously connected in the centre. Gradually these two roughshoots became denuded of pheasants and game by poaching and lack of any real control. Finally, as the roe population increased and the game population with changed farming methods and poaching became almost non-existent, the ground remained basically good roe ground and little else. There are no doubt many other shoots which could show a similar change.

Conversely, of course, there are similar areas which have come under one ownership where a driven shoot has been built up out of what amounted to fairly poor roughshoots, but there the stalking usually remains unchanged. In this instance the stalking was originally a negligible quantity but now is of greater interest and value than the game shooting. In practice there are probably many such shoots where the stalking possibilities are vastly better than a few years back as afforestation continues to spread and roe, fallow and muntjac spread with it ever further, as well as sika and red deer in some places.

The Gralloch

One aspect of deer stalking should be mentioned since the average roughshooter unused to deer may be unaccustomed to it. That is the subject of dealing with the deer once shot. The first thing is to ensure that it is properly bled. The carcase should be laid out on its back on a slope with the head downhill and with the throat exposed. The knife should be inserted in the throat at the junction of neck and chest and the knife blade thrust in and turned thus cutting the arteries to the heart. The knife blade should be at least 4–5 inches (10–12.5 cm). The flow of blood can be accelerated by pumping the hind legs.

The intestines should then be removed. The carcase should first be turned uphill. A fold of skin at the base of the stomach should then be slit and, by inserting a hooked finger and the knife, the skin can be slit, clear of the intestines right up to the rib cage. The same cut can be extended down to the anal passage, but it is first desirable to cut carefully round the anus and ease the contents inwards. If a buck, or stag, the sheath and scrotum should both be cut round at the same time. The aim is to remove the bladder and its contents along with the rest of the intestines without any of them bursting and tainting the meat of the carcase. If the hole cut for bleeding is then widened it is possible to reach in and cut the trachea and oesophagus so that the entire intestines are free at each end and can be tipped onto the ground. It may be necessary to reach in and haul them out and it will certainly be necessary to cut out the liver and remove the kidneys as well as the lungs and heart.

This may well be a bloody business, especially if the beast was shot in the heart or lungs, but the hands may be quickly dried on earth or grass if there is no water nearby to rinse them in. It will then be necessary to empty the accumulated blood from the carcase, but this is usually easily enough done. The liver, kidneys and lights may be put into plastic bags which should be carried for this purpose and the carcase itself should have a short stick thrust across the body cavity to hold it open and allow it to cool as quickly as possible. It is then ready to transport home, but this can sometimes involve a lengthy drag to the car or landrover. Once back it should be hung head up in the larder. The next stage is skinning the carcase after a day or two and jointing it ready for the freezer. The roughshooter stalker has now graduated from dealing with rabbits and hares to bigger things, but the general principle remains the same.

The Close Seasons

		England	Scotland
Fallow	Bucks	1 May–31 July	1 May–31 July
	Does	1 March–31 October	16 February–20 October
Red	Stags	1 May–31 July	21 October–30 June
	Hinds	1 March–31 October	16 February–20 October
Roe	Bucks	1 November–31 March	21 October–31 March
	Does	1 March–31 October	1 August–20 October
Sika	Stags	1 May–31 July	21 October–30 June
	Hinds	1 March–31 October	16 February–20 October
Red Sika	Stags		21 October–30 June
Hybrid	Hinds		16 February–20 October

A close season for Muntjac and Chinese Water Deer is not as yet statutory but the British Deer Society recommends the period 1 March–31 October.

10

Predators, Traps and Trapping

THE BROWN RAT

Habits and Habitat

It is easily forgotten today in many parts of the country that one of the most persistent and cunning of predators on the young of gamebirds and many other birds is the brown rat. These rats are one of the worst enemies of almost any small mammal or bird and also of man. They will eat and foul with their urine and droppings large quantities of stored grain and any other food to which they can gain access. In addition to killing and eating gamebird or poultry chicks they will also steal and eat their eggs. They may be found almost anywhere and can readily adapt to their surroundings.

Size and Adaptability

The dark grey shape of the rat is a very familiar one and easily recognisable. There is very little difference between the sexes and size is extremely variable. They may be as small as 12 inches (31 cm), but also as much as 25 inches (64 cm). I have never personally bothered to weigh any, but I have been told of rats well over 2 lbs (0.9 kg) and some I have killed cannot have been far short of this size. Any rat over $1\frac{1}{2}$ lbs (0.7 kg) must, however, be regarded as a large rat but, as with any bird or beast, to a large extent growth must be governed by the available feeding. Rats in farmyards with plenty of grain available tend to be much larger than rats in the open.

My brother-in-law, who was in the Merchant Navy at one time, assures me that the largest rat he ever saw in a fairly varied experience was one in the cold store of a container ship carrying meat, which he swore was as large as a Jack Russell terrier and covered with a growth of long hair. He claimed that it would kill any other rat that appeared and the crew would deliberately feed it for this reason. Allowing for Mariner's Licence I can well believe it.

Breeding Habits

As well as being extremely cunning and adaptable rats are also extremely prolific. They breed at three months with a gestation period of only three weeks. They may also have a litter every six weeks throughout the year and an average litter is about six to ten, though it may be more. They are both gregarious and promiscuous and at times extremely hard to trap. They are also filthy in their habits and spread numerous diseases from hepatitis to bubonic plague.

At one time amongst the worst and most common of predators, although now mercifully almost absent in some areas, rats leave easily recognised trademarks behind them. Their runs and holes are usually plain enough. The eggs with the ends gnawed ragged and the contents cleanly sucked, the kills partially eaten with the distinctive gnawing teeth marks are fairly unmistakable. Rat droppings too are usually in evidence and it is as well to remember that these dirty beasts pass on extremely unpleasant diseases such as hepatitis so do handle them and their kills with care. If a dog is bitten while killing a rat it is worth disinfecting the bite. I am well aware that many will consider this quite unnecessary, but, trite as it may be to say so, it is better to be safe than sorry.

Fortunately no longer as common as they once were as a result of well-publicised and determined national campaigns and the effectiveness of poisons such as Warfarin, there are still areas, particularly in the west, where they have survived and grown immune to the regular poisons. The danger is that they could readily return to many areas where they have virtually disappeared with a fresh built-in immunity, if precautions are relaxed. Today they can be so easily dealt with that many people have forgotten what a menace the brown rat can be. Drainpipes baited with Warfarin, placed where no dog or cat can get at them are what is required whenever traces of them are discovered.

The days when it was possible for two or three people to go into any barn after dark, armed with torches and sticks, and guarantee to kill half a dozen rats apiece are past. A Jack Russell terrier or similar dog would then provide interesting sport amongst the sacks of grain as rats leaped everywhere in their efforts to escape. Nowadays with vast grain silos and Warfarin everywhere in evidence rats are not so obvious, but it is important to remain vigilant. Rats may not be common in most places, but they could easily return. They have, for instance, in some areas where Warfarin has failed to kill them, adapted to living in fields of oil seed rape and are accordingly even harder to kill. As soon as any traces of them are found it is essential to start laying down Warfarin and trapping in earnest.

THE STOAT

Stoats are still widespread throughout the British Isles. The males are around 14–15 inches (35–38 cm), including a tail of about 4 inches (10 cm), and weigh around 10 ozs (0.3 kg). The females are around 13 inches (33 cm), weighing around 8 ozs (0.2 kg). Apart from their considerably greater size, stoats are readily distinguishable from weasels throughout the year by the black tip to their tails. In summer their coats are normally brown and similar to the weasel's, but in winter they often turn white. This is by no means always the case and the severity or otherwise of the weather seems to have little bearing on it, since in a comparatively mild winter they will sometimes turn white and conversely sometimes in quite hard weather they may retain their summer colouring.

Habits and Habitat

They will normally make their homes in stone walls, hollows in trees or earth banks, or old rabbit holes and similar places. They usually pair early in January or February and their young are born around April or May, usually with from five to ten in a litter. They may on occasion have second litters as young stoats may sometimes be seen as late as September. As with most such matters a good deal probably depends on the weather and the feeding available. The young are born blind and helpless, but after nine days open their eyes and from then on their development is rapid. They will soon be following their mother and taking part with her in hunting expeditions.

They are extremely fast movers, although seldom seen moving at full speed. I have seen one chasing after a rabbit in the centre of a road and steadily catching up with it even though the rabbit was clearly running as fast as it could. They are also very agile and able to climb and jump extremely well. In addition, they are good swimmers and obviously enjoy entering water. They will kill and eat rats and mice, rabbits and hares, including poultry and nesting gamebirds and their chicks, as well as eggs of all kinds and carrion. They will also catch and eat fish.

Although they are often wanton killers and have to be kept under control, it is hard not to admire them at times. They are extremely courageous and if caught alive in a trap a mature stoat will stand up defiantly with bared teeth and raised ruff, like a miniature lion. Within limits they can be tolerated, but too many will soon kill all the game and songbirds in the area. They are not nocturnal, although they will hunt at night, and they hunt by both sight and scent. They will usually kill by seizing their quarry either by the throat, behind the ear or in the nape of the neck. When sated they may merely leave it dead, or just suck some of the blood. Yet although very cunning and clever in many ways, they are, fortunately, very easily trapped.

THE WEASEL

Weasels are a smaller version of the stoat, russet brown without a black tip to their tails. Nor do they change colour in winter. The males are around 11 inches (28 cm), including a tail of about $2\frac{1}{2}$ inches (6 cm) without a black tip to it. They weigh about $3\frac{1}{2}$ ozs (0.13 kg). The females are nearer 9 inches (23 cm) including a tail of about 2 inches (5 cm) also without a black tip. They will weigh around 3 ounces (0.1 kg). They will have two or even three litters a year, of around four to six or seven in a litter. The first litter is usually born around April or May.

Habits and Habitat

Although they may occasionally kill gamebird chicks they do more good by killing rats, voles and mice, as well as young rabbits. Most countrymen will have seen them steadily pursuing a rabbit until the beast becomes almost hypnotised and is easily killed in the same manner as by the stoat with a bite in the nape of the neck, or throat. Watching the young weasels playing with their mother is an enchanting spectacle as they twine round each other in the open, rolling and twisting, or run up and down a wall or trunk of a tree. They are fascinating creatures to watch and like stoats are very courageous. They tend to live in similar sorts of places to stoats, but being smaller can follow mice down their runs and enter similar tiny nooks and crannies. They are very agile and good swimmers, but do not climb or swim as readily as stoats. Most shoots can stand them within reasonable numbers. Again they are very easily trapped.

MINK

Mink are decidedly different. These thoroughly bloodthirsty killers have nothing to recommend them. They will kill almost anything and attack without warning. They are capable of killing small pet dogs or puppies, and also cats. A large mink may be close to a full grown cat in size, but most are of a similar size to ferrets. Their normal habitat is close to water, but they tend to wander considerable distances, especially during the mating season. Then a male mink will mark out his own distinctive territory.

Habits and Habitat

Mink were first introduced from North America in the 1920s when they were farmed for their valuable pelts. With a steady increase in the number of mink farms there were inevitably a number of escapes. First reports of them breeding in the wild were from Devon in the mid-1950s. Some were probably deliberately released in 1962 when mink farming regulations were tightened up. More recently there have been attacks on mink farms by animal liberation fanatics when considerable numbers have been deliberately set loose in the wild. Most of these have either soon been recovered, or have perished miserably, but a few may have adapted and survived to become a menace to the wildlife population as a whole. The net result is that they are now very firmly established throughout most of the country and have become a considerable threat to other wildlife. Although usually encountered near streams, lakes and rivers they can also travel considerable distances across any ground and may be found miles from any water.

   While they may be found in many colour variations, they generally revert in the wild in course of time to near black with white chin and coat. Their pelts are useless for furs in the spring, or for that matter in the autumn as they are invariably scratched and torn in the wild. They have thus little value and should never be deliberately left until autumn, for by that time they will have bred and denuded the ground of game anyway. They are expert fishers and are a constant threat to fisheries as well as game farms, or ordinary shoots, since they are even more wanton killers than stoats. They will deliberately kill large numbers of poults or fish, should they manage to find an unguarded release pen or fish tank, and will store them in a carefully concealed spot nearby, often not bothering to return to their cache, which may only be discovered in due course by the smell of rotting flesh.

Unfortunately unlike stoats and weasels, which may be killed by cats, owls, buzzards and foxes, mink have no natural predators in the British Isles and can live for up to seven years. Like the stoat and weasel they normally mate from February to April, producing litters of from three to seven. Although they hunt by both day and night they are not often seen. Apart from their tracks, the first sign of their presence may be a sudden diminution in the numbers of moorhens and voles seen in the area, since these are amongst their favourite and easiest prey. Their distinctive star shaped tracks too will be found in muddy places, but should not be confused with an otter's, which are appreciably larger.

Luckily, since they have no predators to fear and perhaps following years of artificial rearing, they have apparently no inborn fear of man. They are easily enough caught in cage traps, or in specially powerful spring traps. If these are placed at intersections, such as tributary streams, or minor drains, or under banks, where mink are likely to travel, they are comparatively easily caught. Once a trap has proved successful it will usually catch several more and, if left, will continue to do so. Several such traps may be successful in catching a number at the same time.

THE FOX

Another serious headache to the game preserver, but at least a native of these islands and one to which we have become accustomed, is the fox. Common throughout the British Isles, they are well known, with their distinctive triangular heads, russet coats and noticeably bushy tails, or brushes. Foxes may vary in weight from around 10–12 lbs (4.5–5.5 kg) up to as much as 20 lbs (9 kg), or even 25 lbs (11 kg). The dog and vixen normally live apart except during the breeding season in the spring. During the mating season several dog foxes may follow one vixen and they may be heard barking before she chooses a mate. By imitating the bark it is possible to call a fox within gunshot and I have accounted for a number in this way. It is also simple enough to call them within shot by imitating the call of a wounded or snared rabbit. Good calls can be bought for this purpose and can be very effective.

Habits and Habitat

They are mainly nocturnal aninmals, living in an earth, which may be freshly dug, or adapted from a disused rabbit burrow, or even sharing part of a badger's den. The earths are usually easily identified by smell, or by traces of kills around the entrance, or by the tracks or other traces of the adults and cubs. The litters may vary in size from two to as many as six or eight and even more have been known. The cubs are born blind, but fully furred, and open their eyes within about nine days. The vixen will move her earth at once if she thinks it has been discovered. The dog fox who has mated with her will usually stay on hand to help to feed the young.

They are extremely cunning and eat a wide variety of food from gamebirds, poultry, rats, lambs, even sheep if weakly, and it is alleged that they have accounted for New Forest pony foals. They will also, however, eat fish, frogs and snakes, as well as berries and fruits. They will scavenge widely on carrion and in towns, where many have adapted to an urban existence, will knock the tops off dustbins to forage through their contents.

In the country they are a persistent enemy of the game preserver, who may trap and shoot them, but will generally rely more on snaring them. Where there is a local hunt he will look to their help in killing them also and there are few more instant deaths for a fox than being killed by hounds. The first one up simply snaps the spine and the fox dies instantly. I have seen this at close quarters and there can be few more immediate deaths. Many areas, however, have no hunts and here the roughshooter must adopt his own methods of keeping them under control.

THE GREY SQUIRREL

Another troublesome predator on many roughshoots may be the grey squirrel, or Tree Rat as they are sometimes called since the two species have much in common. This is another introduced species which has become a pest. Throughout much of England and parts

of southern Scotland grey squirrels have driven the native red species
from the ground and are continuing their northward spread. Unlike
red squirrels the greys, have nothing to recommend them, beyond
the fact that they are surprisingly good eating, if sometimes rather
tiresome to skin, and their tails are useful for tying flies for fishing.

Habits and Habitat

Like rats, the sexes are similar in appearance and size. Their normal
weight is around $1\frac{1}{2}$ lbs (0.7 kg). They have from three to five young
in a litter and from two to three litters in a year. They will breed at
a year old and live in dreys, or domed nests, covered in twigs in the
treetops. They will also live, or shelter, in hollow trees and the roofs
of outhouses or similar sites, including, it is said, rabbit burrows.

They are destructive eaters, living on buds, nuts, fruit and vegetables as well as any kind of birds' eggs and they also kill and eat
the young birds themselves. Like rats they may be poisoned with
Warfarin and this is one of the methods used against them, using a
hopper of poisoned bait firmly pegged in position to about every 10
acres (4 ha). These hoppers should be set in the trees at shoulder
height or thereabouts to prevent other animals upsetting them or
sampling them by accident and they should be inspected regularly.
In areas where there are still red squirrels (including all of Scotland)
this method is illegal.

Squirrels are not easy to shoot, but may be stalked and shot with
a .22 rifle. They may also be trapped in cage traps, or in snares. As
with rats, all-out-war should be waged against them. They should
be regarded as high on the list of predators which should be trapped
or shot whenever possible.

THE POLECAT

There are sundry other four-legged predators, which the average
roughshooter is unlikely ever to encounter and which anyway are
protected, but which should perhaps be mentioned in case he does
run across them. Amongst these are the polecat, which may be met
with in Wales and the West Midlands. Any polecats encountered in
Scotland are in fact feral ferrets and may be controlled in the usual
manner. The polecat is a very large and strong-smelling black stoat.
The males are about 30 inches (76 cm) long, of which about 8 inches

(20 cm) is tail, and they weigh about $2\frac{3}{4}$ lbs (1.25 kg). The females are about 26 inches (66 cm) long, of which about 6 inches (15 cm) is tail, and they weigh about $1\frac{3}{4}$ lbs (0.8 kg). Polecats are mainly found in woods, especially in hilly country. They are mainly nocturnal and their principal quarry is rabbits, but they will also take gamebirds and poultry. They are also good swimmers and will catch fish. They are courageous and fierce, but are easily trapped. They are partially protected under the Wildlife and Countryside Act of 1981. It is legal to shoot them but they may not be trapped.

THE PINE MARTEN

The once even rarer pine marten is now becoming much more common north of Inverness with the increasing afforestation of the Highlands. It looks like a very large stoat, with a mature male measuring 34 inches (86 cm) of which 12 inches (30 cm) is tail. They may weigh up to $3\frac{1}{2}$ lbs (1.6 kg). They are usually found only in very thick woodland or rocky hillsides, and are extremely wild. They will take rabbits, squirrels, voles, snakes and all birds, including poultry, but will also eat wasps and berries. They are easy to trap, but are strictly protected under the 1981 Wildlife and Countryside Act.

THE WILDCAT

The true wildcat, only to be found in parts of the Scottish Highlands and north-east Lowlands, is also protected. Recognisable by its remarkable bushy tail, it hunts principally at dawn and dusk. It is carnivorous and will attack almost anything if cornered, but chiefly lives on rabbits, hares and grouse. It will mate willingly with domestic cats, but because of its scarcity it is protected. The feral domestic cat, however, which has taken to living on the countryside is possibly amongst the most common and most lethal menaces to game, or for that matter any songbirds, to be found and should be trapped, shot or otherwise disposed of whenever possible. It is sometimes difficult to distinguish between a pet cat which has been abandoned by callous owners and one that is the apple of its owner's eye, but it should be remembered that pet cats are property and under the Theft Act 1968 it is illegal to kill them.

The Badger

The badger is also rightly protected and the roughshooter who is fortunate enough to have some on his ground will find they are delightful animals to watch. They should never be harmed in any way. An occasional rogue badger may get into a hen-run and prove troublesome, while now and then a pheasant nest may be taken, leaving a mess of ruined egg shells as evidence. In the main, however, badgers are quite harmless neighbours.

The only occasion they may be troublesome is when they blunder into a badly set fox snare and wind themselves round with wire in their efforts to escape. A pair of powerful wire cutters should be carried for such occasions, since unwinding them is not likely to be easy. It may be possible to hold them down with a booted foot, or a forked stick cut from a tree, while releasing them, but it is not easy with their powerful jaws.

Fortunately this is a situation I have encountered only once, when I had a companion with me. Then I held the half-suffocated old sow very firmly by the loose folds of skin at the scruff of the neck with both hands while my companion unwound the wire. She then departed at a fast waddle with a parting pat on the backside, not having attempted to struggle or bite, possibly because she was aware she was being helped, but more probably because she was already exhausted by her efforts to free herself. That is not, however, a course to be recommended with a powerful struggling boar badger.

THE HEDGEHOG

Another animal which can be tiresome by frequently getting itself caught in traps is the hedgehog. This is another animal which is partly protected by the 1981 Wildlife Act, although undoubtedly quite often guilty of egg stealing. With their inquisitive noses and prickly spines the hedge-pig as it is known in some places, rootles around the ground in a very pig-like manner at times. They will sometimes snort quite loudly and when asleep may snore. Probably their most tiresome habit, however, is blundering into the game preservers' traps despite efforts to prevent this.

Trapping

Rats and other small ground predators may be caught in ordinary approved humane spring traps, of which there is only one type now being manufactured in various forms, the Fenn. When setting such traps, of course, it is essential to place them where no other animal, such as a dog, or a cat, or any bird, may be caught in them. It is illegal to set any trap in the open where this might happen. They must be covered. Tunnel traps are the usual method employed to make sure that a trap is selective. Tunnel traps, as the name implies, are simply traps set under the cover of a man-made tunnel.

Tunnel Traps

Tunnel traps may be of a great many materials and designs, since the principle is simply to ensure that the trap is covered. The simplest type are made from a suitable covering, such as a draining tile or plank of wood, merely leaning against a wall at an angle so as to allow a small predator access. They may also be made much more elaborately. For instance, in a suitable place where tracks indicate the presence of predators a trench may be made and covered with a natural looking roof. Alternatively a tunnel might be built up with bricks and roofed over with a piece of timber, tin, or any other material to hand. To get the best results it is important to make the tunnel just the right width and height to suit the trap. When the tunnel is too large the intended victims may be thrown free, becoming very 'trap-shy' as a result.

The main feature of a tunnel trap is that it should be placed where ground predators, such as rats, stoats, weasels or mink are likely to be found. If there are runs indicating their presence the ideal is to set such tunnel traps on these runs, or in the close vicinity of them. Most small predators have an instinctive urge to investigate any such tunnels or likely holes they may encounter, and an attractive pathway may be made to lead them towards the trap.

Sticking the Tunnels

It has already been pointed out that other creatures, such as hedgehogs, indeed especially hedgehogs, also have an interest in investigating such tunnels. In order to prevent hedgehogs, inquisitive poults or similar such enquiring innocents, from being caught in tunnel traps it is always advisable to insert a couple of sticks in the ground at the entrance to prevent anything entering except the predators it is intended to catch. This is known as 'sticking' the tunnel trap and is an important precaution to remember, although not always successful in the case of determined hedgehogs.

Access to the Traps

It is also necessary to have easy access to the tunnel for various reasons, such as checking the traps, removing any victims or re-setting them. It should therefore be easy to remove the covering, or lid, so as to get at the traps. Since it usually takes a little time and trouble to build a good tunnel trap it is generally worth making it large enough to hold two traps, one at each end. It thus has a double chance of being effective and ideally may claim a victim at each end. In fact often the presence of one victim may draw another to investigate, which is in turn caught by the second trap. Where the tunnel trap is long enough this also allows room for a bait to be placed in the centre inside the tunnel to excite the interest of the intended victims and draw them to it.

Re-Setting

Quite apart from being able to examine the traps easily, it is desirable to be able to re-set them easily when a victim has been claimed without disturbing the entire tunnel. Furthermore, traps should not be left set too long and it is desirable to examine them and re-set them at intervals to ensure that they have not rusted, or become jammed with earth or mud. It is incidentally always advisable to check any trap which does not seem to have been successful for a few days, since it is easy for a novice or an absent-minded trapper to leave the safety catch in place after putting the trap in position. Even experienced trappers have been known to make this mistake occasionally. In the case of a baited tunnel trap it is also necessary to be able to open the trap to see whether the bait requires renewing. It is also desirable to ensure that the bait has not been removed with the trap unaffected.

Approved Traps

It is important only to use the approved spring traps, all now manufactured by Fenn. The Fenn Mark IV is only for rats and small ground predators but the Fenn Mark VI general-purpose trap is for predators up to the size of mink and rabbits. It is no use using the Fenn Mark IV trap for mink. It simply is not strong enough. The Juby trap, now no longer manufactured, although many are still around, has particularly powerful jaws, which require a foot lever to help open it. It has such a strong action that it is quite capable of killing rabbits and mink, but it requires a split tunnel, or larger tunnel or opening, to allow room for the jaws to operate.

Removing Scent Traces

In setting any trap, whether inside a hole or in a tunnel, naturally enough, it is essential that all smell of man should be removed. Before setting any trap it is well worth smearing it with earth freshly taken from the top soil. Loose friable earth such as is found in the top of a molehill is ideal. Before starting, this should also be rubbed over the hands to remove the smell of human sweat or possibly soap, which will otherwise taint the traps.

The same principle applies to the objects used in making the tunnel trap. They should all be smeared with soil, or be sufficiently weathered to have lost all traces of scent of man. Many keepers advise burying new traps for a week or two before use for the same reason. This is probably unnecessary, although it can do no harm. At the same time, while it is desirable to test that the trap is in working order from time to time it is not desirable to oil them or interfere with them beyond ensuring that the spring action is functioning effectively. If they do require lubrication use lard or vegetable oil, not mineral oils.

Cage Traps

Cage traps are also available for taking most ground predators alive. For mink these must be strong 14-gauge weldmesh or heavier without any wood showing, as a mature mink will soon eat its way through any wood and will chew through any lighter wire comparatively easily. It should be added that when caught in a cage trap mink make a considerable commotion. It should therefore be firmly pegged in place or it may roll some distance from where it was placed. Several such cage traps side by side may each catch separate members of the same mink family.

Baits

On well-proven sites cage traps may not even need to be baited and mink will still enter them just the same. Almost anything such as rabbit heads, fish heads or offal is likely to prove effective as bait if it is felt necessary, but whatever is used should be fresh. The body of a freshly killed stoat or other predator, itself may often prove a strong attraction for a mate or relative. The twin lures of food and sex are usually effective in luring any ground predators and sometimes, for instance, a long trail may be laid by dragging the dead body of a female, or some fresh rabbit guts, as a lure towards a cage trap, or spring trap set in a tunnel.

Despatching the Predator

Once caught in a spring trap, despatching the predator humanely with a loaded priest or stick is simple. When caught in a cage trap it is not so simple. Mink especially are fierce and fearless as well as being armed with long canines. For this reason cage traps designed for mink are provided with a carrying handle and they can, of course, be submerged, but since mink can swim well this is not particularly quick or humane. One solution which is very effective is to insert the barrel of a loaded air rifle into the cage and when the mink seizes this firmly in its jaws turn it so that it is aimed at the brain and pull the trigger.

The Bender

The old and tried methods of trapping and snaring are always hard to beat when any predators are proving troublesome. Amongst the first of these is the age-old bender, which is especially effective against rats. Where the rat runs are plain, as they usually are, a bender is likely to prove a most satisfactory method of trapping. The bender, as the name suggests, is a bent wand of hazel wood attached to a wire snare and inserted deeply in the ground. It is then bent over so that the snare may be set to dangle directly over the run. It is held in position by a taut wire or cord, from another stake set in the ground, and two interlocking wooden pegs hold the bender taut. As soon as any lateral strain is put on the snare the two pegs fly apart and the hazel wand straightens so that the victim is swung aloft to dangle with the snare around his neck, to die instantly of a broken neck, or quickly from loss of air. The principle of the bender on a larger scale has been used in mantraps and to catch quarry as large as bears. The principle can be applied to almost any snare for any beast.

Checking Traps

By law all traps must be checked once in twenty-four hours. Many trappers will prefer to check their traps morning and evening at intervals of twelve hours. It is largely a question of how much time is available. A full-time keeper with a 1,500 acre shoot might run from 70–100 traps fairly comfortably. If he is rearing birds he may not have time for more. If no birds are reared it may be necessary to set more to protect sitting birds.

On the whole, the part-time keeper on the roughshoot will do well if he can cover 500 acres or so thoroughly. In any event he would be well-advised to have numerous tunnel traps prepared and vary his trapping amongst different areas of the shoot, so that he can trap one area intensively over a short period and then move his traps to a different ground. In this way he should manage to cover the entire ground very thoroughly on a rota system. This is probably better than spreading his efforts over a wider area and not achieving such good results. The important feature of setting traps for ground predators is being able to recognise the signs left by the various predators and knowing where to look for them. There is considerable satisfaction to be had from a successful trap round.

The Problems of the Part-Time Trapper

The part-time roughshoot game preserver and trapper has different problems from the full-time keeper. He may only have time once a week to set his traps on the Saturday morning and check them that evening and the following morning, with a final check on the Sunday evening when all have to be unset or removed. Making sure that traps do not go astray is a problem even for professional keepers. It is important to have tunnel traps sited so that although they are obvious to the predators and attractive to them they remain inconspicuous to any chance passers-by, who might be tempted to investigate them and, from malice or simply lack of understanding, or just for reasons of plain theft, remove them.

Thinking Small

When trapping small ground predators it is necessary to think in miniature. The signs of tiny tracks and movements are there and the trapper simply has to think small. To encourage the predators to move in the required direction it may be necessary to erect a barrier of twigs, or simply dig an artificial route, or lay a trail of interesting scent, using the lures of either greed or sex. Once the trapper has learned the problems and experienced the satisfactions, he will find a trap round can be immensely interesting and satisfying as well as quite infuriating at times.

Fox Snares

Setting fox snares is a last resort in some ways, as they cannot always be humane, but they can prove very effective, and the more skilled the trapper is the more humane they will be. For a start, only free-running snares are legal and the object should always be to ensure catching foxes only and to kill them as cleanly as possible. Fox snares should be set normally about six inches (15 cm) above ground unless in the open when they might be 8 inches (20 cm) high. The wire should be pear shaped and about 6 inches (15 cm) deep and 8 inches (21 cm) across.

A stop should be fixed on the snare, a screw or a few turns of wire, about 7 inches (20 cm) from the eye so that any animal, such as a deer or sheep, putting a leg through it will not be caught accidentally. To prevent deer being caught a jump bar may be erected consisting simply of a stout branch supported on a couple of forked sticks a few centimetres above the snare. If this is not set too high it should persuade the deer to leap the obstacle rather than go under it.

As with a rabbit snare, the wire loop will need to be supported by a wooden tealer, or support, split at the top, into which the wire fits. In very windy positions two tealers may be required to hold the wire steady. The snare itself should be secured to something heavy such as a log or stob, which will act as a drag. The captive fox will then bolt for the nearest cover and should be found at dawn and shot. Snares should be set late in the evening and inspected at dawn and any captives humanely shot at once. If set in well-marked runs the success rate should be high, but a gun at dawn, or better still rifle, may well result in as many being shot as snared.

WINGED PREDATORS

So far the trapper has only been concerned with outwitting the four-legged predators. Unfortunately on most shoots winged predators, especially egg thieves, are almost certainly every bit as much of a problem. All corvids, rooks, crows, both carrion and hooded, jackdaws and magpies may be included amongst the most accomplished egg thieves and where there are too many of any of these species on the shoot they should be controlled in one way or another. Shooting or decoying, with shotgun and rifle is one way of dealing with any or all of them, and if numbers are small, the more obvious offenders can be dealt with individually in this way.

Cage Traps

A cage trap, working on the funnel and lobster pot principle, made of wire netting some 6 × 6 × 6 feet with an opening in the top, if well placed, will soon prove its worth. If it has an opening on ground level as well this may bring in additional birds and sometimes also catch squirrels. The snag is that it may also sometimes catch game. Such traps may be baited with some fresh rabbit guts and will soon attract birds. Cage traps work best if the roof is left off and they are pre-baited for a week or so. In this way the entire flock is usually caught and not just a few. It is essential, however, that any birds caught are killed, since if they are released not only will they never be caught again, but they will warn all their fellows about the dangers of the trap and it will remain useless until moved.

Whatever type of trapping is involved, the part-time trapper will be improving his shoot by removing some of the predators of game. In learning the ways of the predators and also the ways of the game itself, he will learn a great deal about his ground. Every day out on his trap round should teach him something useful, even if it is only that animals are often a great deal cleverer than humans would believe possible.

11

The Dog on the Roughshoot

On the Moorland Roughshoot

The dog on the roughshoot can literally mean the difference between good sport and poor sport or no sport at all. On the moorland roughshoot the dog must be a wide-ranging point-retriever, covering the ground, hunting it thoroughly and finding and pointing the game. Without a dog of this nature the sport will be minimal. The spaniel working within range of the gun will be comparatively useful, but vast acreages of the ground simply will not be covered and the game, if it is there at all, will not be found nearly as readily. Walking up such extensive ground is seldom practical.

On the Low Ground Roughshoot

On the low ground shoot a great deal again depends on the dog. Here the wide-ranging pointer-retriever may again be useful on the open grass fields and stubbles, where game may be lying tight or moving on ahead. In the root fields, in the gorse and whins, the spaniel may come into its own and the wide-ranging dog must be taught to curb its range or else be brought in to heel. If the guns are simply walking up in line with their dogs at heel instead of working in front they may well have quite good sport, but game will almost certainly be missed. The perfect retriever, which always marches at heel and only goes forward when its master tells it to do so, certainly may be useful, but in these circumstances this is limiting the owner's chances of sport.

The Breed of Dog

On the roughshoot the breed of dog scarcely matters as long as it will hunt and has a good nose. I have known dogs of almost every breed as well as cross-breeds, which worked well as long-range pointer-retrievers, or as short-range pointer-retrievers, or bustling the game up within range like spaniels. The essence of all gundog work lies in co-operation between handler and dog and in mutual understanding of what is required. When the aim is to find game on the ground and to shoot it, the dog and handler should work in a harmonious partnership and with complete understanding of what is required. They must also understand the ways of the game likely to be encountered and what their own part in the proceedings should be.

I had one old dog who, if I missed several times in succession, very obviously took a poor view of it and was liable to peg the next game encountered as if to ensure that there was something in the bag. On one occasion after six successive misses he gave me a devastatingly scornful look and turned for home regardless of my whistle. I had to admit that I saw his point, but I felt it was carrying canine criticism too far.

Mutual Understanding

The question of when a dog and man reach an equal partnership is, of course, a delicate one. Some dogs are born with an instinctive understanding of what is required and can teach their handler from the earliest days, if he is sensible enough to realise it. Other dogs will always welcome a little assistance and encouragement, but may make good enough working dogs. Some handlers will never understand what it is all about and that is that. It is basically a question of instinctive understanding, not only of what part each should play, but also of how the game is likely to react and how to circumvent it.

Understanding the Ways of Game

A natural feeling for dogs is not in itself enough. The handler who would take his dog out roughshooting first of all has to understand the behaviour and likely reactions of the game on the ground over which he is shooting, having regard to the wind and weather conditions. He also has to be able to shoot it once the dog has successfully found it, whether or not it was where they expected it to be. Each member of the partnership has to play his part. When the dog is scolded unfairly for some reason he may well not have understood, then it is understandable if he subsequently refuses to obey orders. The handler must always try to look at events from the dog's viewpoint as well as his own.

The Requirements

This may sound as if I am starting this chapter at the wrong end, but that is not so. Before choosing his dog and even considering what breed of dog he should have, the roughshooter must decide what he wants the dog to do. To a large extent this must be dictated by his shooting and the ground over which he chiefly shoots. It is pointless having a wide-ranging dog suitable for large fields and moorland if he only has a shoot of small stubble fields and woodland strips. Equally a short-legged close-ranging dog is not the dog for sweeping downland or moorland. Once he has clear in his mind the type of dog he requires, he may go ahead and choose the breed he thinks will suit his purpose best. In practice almost all dogs can work effectively on a roughshoot if they are handled by a man who knows what to expect from them and if they have the initial working abilities in them. It is astonishing how few people buy a dog with any clear conception either of what they want it for or what its background breeding might lead them to expect. That many people get good working dogs is often more than they deserve.

Breeding

Ideally if you are choosing a dog, rather than breeding your own, you should see the parents working, or have first hand reports on them, by unbiased observers. Too many people think the sun shines only on their dog and fail to see its shortcomings. They breed from it and perpetuate trouble. Others genuinely do not realise that if you breed a small fat bitch with bow legs to a long-legged rangy dog you will not necessarily get a happy mean. You may end up with a long lean body and short legs, or a short fat body and long legs. Either way, there is no guarantee that any working abilities on either side will be passed on, since haphazard breeding has a habit of producing haphazard results.

Good Working Stock

It cannot be repeated too often that it is worth paying a reasonable sum for a dog of sound working stock on both sides, which has been bred by people who know what they are about. The chances are rather more than even then that the results will prove satisfactory. Thereafter, if the dog or bitch is satisfactory it is well worth trying to perpetuate the bloodline, by breeding from it if a bitch or using it as a sire on a suitable bitch if a dog. Again, if you do not know about breeding, then consult a reputable breeder of the breed concerned. D.I.Y. backyard dog-breeding almost always ends in trouble.

Game finding Abilities

Whatever the breed, whether naturally a retriever, such as a golden retriever or labrador, it should, if it is to be worked on the roughshoot as a game finder, be taught to work ahead of the guns to find game. If it is to be worked well out beyond the immediate range of the guns it must be taught to halt on finding game and if not freezing rigidly like a trained pointer, at least to stand with tail gently waving until the handler arrives within range. It is perfectly feasible to train any dog on these lines and the only advantage of the pointer-retriever breeds for this sort of work is that it tends to be bred into them. The training should thus be simpler when it comes to hunting, finding game and pointing. The dogs should also be sound retrievers, but naturally on the retrieving side the retrieving breeds have that bred into them so that for them little or no training should be required in that aspect.

Working Within Range of the Gun

If the handler wishes always to work his dog within range of a gun on a roughshoot then a spaniel is supposedly bred for this purpose. In fact many long-legged spaniels are more akin to setters, ranging wide and coming on quite a firm point when game is found. Training any dog to work within range of the gun is always something of a problem, but again if the handler perseveres, any type of dog, whether retriever, pointer-retriever, spaniel or setter, can be taught to work within range and push up game. The only problem usually is that when taught to work in this way it is not always easy to get such a dog to work far out when required to do so. Nor, it should be pointed out, should any dog be expected to work in this very demanding fashion in its first season. It is always important to take time over the training.

The Learning Process for the Dog

It is very easy, especially with a precocious youngster which seems to be a natural worker to push it far too hard too soon. There is no quicker way of ruining a gundog and it is usually those with most promise that are spoiled in this way. To train a dog to work efficiently on the roughshoot is not the work of one season or even two. It should be regarded as a continuous process and sadly it is often only as the dog is beginning to be past his prime that he can truthfully be said to be starting to know it all.

The Learning Process for the Trainer

Before the roughshooter buys his first pup he would be well advised to buy a good book on gundog training. This will usually start by advising him on how to choose a pup and he should start by reading the book right through. He should then have some idea of where to start and what to expect. Alternatively, if there are reliable training classes available, he may well decide to attend these with his dog. It is only if he knows what he is intending to do that he can possibly succeed in training a gundog. Only if he knows what he wants and how to set about getting it is he likely to choose the right pup.

Obviously no one is likely to train a dog successfully unless they fully understand what they want it to do and have a fairly clear idea of how to set about persuading it to do whatever is required. As well as indicating the various stages step by step a good guide to gundog training should also indicate the likely mistakes and the possible reactions of the dog. The ultimate success or failure of the exercise, however, lies with the handler, although a really outstanding dog can sometimes go a long way towards training an inexperienced handler. If he perseveres and the dog proves a ready pupil he may even find that ultimately he has achieved that most satisfying of results, an almost telepathic understanding and communication between man and dog.

The Training Process

Training any dog has it moments of profound satisfaction and its moments of deepest gloom, when all seems to have gone wrong. In practice, if the trainer will only persevere and not press matters too hard, which is the usual novice error, it very often all works out in a surprising way and his efforts will pay off in the end. The novice who has successfully trained his own first gundog is, of course, seldom likely to acknowledge its faults, but even if it commits numerous heinous crimes he will probably be enormously pleased with it and should himself have learned a great deal in the process.

The Pleasures of Success

There are few more heart-warming moments for any roughshooter than seeing the dog he has trained coming back successfully with a strong runner after a seemingly impossible retrieve. Only when he has bred the dog himself and it has hunted the ground, found and pointed the game in the first place is he likely to feel any greater satisfaction. When the roughshooter's dog is successful in every aspect of its work, when it will hunt either close at hand or wide, depending on the ground, when it will find and hold the game, before flushing and retrieving it on command, and when he has bred it himself, each day out is pure delight.

The Hard Cases

There are those, of course, who should never handle dogs at all and who will ruin any dog they own. It is difficult to convince such people that they should not try to train a dog. Even when they buy a dog ready trained, or have their own dog trained professionally, the results are never satisfactory. The inability to stick to firm simple commands, a constant nervousness in case the dog does something wrong, a stream of contrary orders, whistles and curses, all these are signs of the confirmed non-dog-minded owner, who is unfortunately only too common. There is very little that can be done to help such confirmed cases or their dogs. Training classes may help to some extent, but although some training classes are indeed well run and very helpful, sometimes they are a case of the blinkered leading the blind, and really bad cases are anyway usually past help.

The Training Choices

In anything to do with dogs and their training it is best to try to keep an open mind, but it is not always easy. There will be those who swear by rabbit skins on their dummies. Others will maintain earnestly that a pair of pigeon wings sewn to the dummy are the only way to start. Yet others may argue that a pigeon inside a length of nylon stocking, or a piece of car hose covered with canvas and weighted with sand are best for a pup to start its retrieving. On the whole it is surprising that any dog survives the often amazing training methods inflicted on them and still succeeds in working tolerably well and sometimes even excellently. It says much for the dogs, if not perhaps a great deal for their handlers.

The Dog's Viewpoint

The simple explanation for this is that the dog is much more single-minded than his handler. The dog does not have so much on his mind. He is not thinking about the stock market, or what his wife is going to say about them being late yet again, or whether that last consignment from Hungary will arrive on time. The dog is concentrating on the scents of game and the sound of his handler's whistle, but he may well be ready to run after a tempting rabbit moving ahead of him if he is not checked with a cautionary warning in time. The handler has to be constantly on the alert too, or he is simply not playing his part and cannot expect the dog to play his.

The Handler's Viewpoint

As when driving a car, the roughshooter working his dog should be regarding the ground ahead on two levels. On the one hand he should be thinking where the game is likely to be and working his dog primarily in that direction. He should also be thinking of what will happen when the game is found and be ready to caution his dog if he shows signs of running in over eagerly and possibly flushing the game out of shot. He should then be ready for the game to be flushed and be prepared to pick his shots and mark the fall of game. At the same time he should be watching his dog and making sure he does not run in to flush or fall.

Working without the Gun

It is easy to make mistakes. Too much concentration on either dog or shooting may result in frustration. Either the roughshooter misses a simple shot clean to his annoyance, or the dog runs in regardless, also to the roughshooter's annoyance. A common solution is that the roughshooter accustoms himself to shooting the game and allowing his dog to run in to fetch it willy-nilly, for want of the ability to do anything to stop it. The alternative is to give the dog sufficient training early on to ensure that he drops to shot. This means working the dog without a gun to start with, a discipline which many people will not follow. It should not in fact require very long to get the message across, but of course it must be reinforced from time to time and, if the dog runs in subsequently when the roughshooter is concentrating on the shooting, he should go back to letting his friends take the shot while he gives the dog a refresher lesson.

Providing Early Experience

Before ever taking the dog out on the shoot it is essential to try to prepare him for as many of the pitfalls he is likely to encounter as possible. For instance, once he has learned to retrieve dummies to order, it is desirable to train him to follow a scent trail. This is easily enough done by laying a trail with the dummy, or if he has reached the stage of retrieving game, with freshly-shot game. By watching him follow this a very good idea will be formed of the dog's scenting abilities. After the first few have been followed successfully more difficult trails may be laid, with breaks here and there forcing the dog to cast round to find the scent again. By assisting him at these points the handler can implant the message that theirs is a working partnership in which each has a role to play. Nor should the trainer expect the dog to work perfectly on low ground, when it has only worked on grouse on the moor, or vice versa. The dog will naturally require as much experience of all types of game as can be obtained before he can be expected to fulfil his role as an all-round working dog.

A Quick Way to Ruin the Dog

Without considerable preparatory training before working in the field no dog can seriously be expected to perform properly. If the dog is pitched straight in at the deep end and is merely taken out with the gun and expected to work then the handler will get all he deserves. The dog may become gun shy, or at least gun nervous, through not having been properly introduced to the gun. Alternatively, never having been subjected to proper initial obedience training it may simply run wild, a nuisance to all, until its handler puts it on the lead, when it will probably pull him off his balance at intervals and prove a thorough nuisance to him. Such a dog cannot be expected to have anything but a hard mouth, crunching game whenever it is allowed the opportunity, and it will almost certainly refuse to retrieve to hand, if it will bring it at all. However strong its instincts may be, a dog must have initial training before being taken into the field, or it will quickly be completely ruined. Yet this sort of thing is still occasionally seen. There are still people who think their dog's instincts are so strong that there is no need for training and the dog will simply train itself. They will soon find that without a thorough basic training in obedience no gundog, however strong his instincts may be, can possibly work well.

Knowing the Reactions of Game

In training a dog for roughshooting, far more so than when training a dog for driven shooting, it is essential to know the reactions of game at all times. Even when training a retriever it is highly desirable to know the ways of shot game. It is only by being able to interpret accurately the behaviour of game on the ground, or when shot, that it is possible to understand and if necessary correct the dog's reactions. It is only by knowing what the game is likely to be doing and where it will probably be at any given time of the day, that a dog's movements as he covers the ground can be correctly followed and understood. That pause when he put his nose down was where the covey of partridges had been. That quick run along the hedge was where the cock pheasant ran along before slipping through into the next field. Only when this stage has been reached can a useful word of caution, or helpful signal, be given in the right place at the right moment.

Working Harmony

It is a pleasure to watch a well matched and experienced dog and handler working together. The dog will hunt its ground systematically, clearly passing information to its handler with a brief check here and a turn of the head there and answering to a barely perceptible whistle and signal from him with scarcely a pause. Once this supremely satisfying working harmony has been achieved, with dog and handler each instinctively responding to the other, while studying the ground ahead, each day out becomes a pleasure to them both. The roughshooter who has once trained a dog to this standard will obtain enormous satisfaction from his sport.

Marking Towered Birds

If a bird is seen to be flying steadily higher and higher it was almost certainly hit in the lung or spine and will continue to fly higher with arching back striving for air as its lungs fill with blood. It will then suddenly collapse in mid-flight, falling straight downward and frequently landing on its back. The roughshooter may see it thus tower and fall as much as several hundred yards and a couple of fields away. He will have crouched automatically to try to get a background marker for the fall and will have done his best to estimate the range. He will then memorise the markers. Thus when he goes forward with his dog he will know where to stop and when to send the dog forward to around the estimated fall. To go too far would be to foul the ground for the dog and by casting the dog downwind he knows that he is giving it every chance of catching the scent and going straight to the fall. He will know that sometimes for no particularly obvious reason such birds have virtually no scent. He will not therefore be too disturbed if he himself spots the bird and sees his dog walk straight over it without apparently scenting it.

Marking Hit Birds

If a bird is seen to flinch to shot, but does not fall, it is always worth following its flight as far as the eye can see. The chances are high that it will suddenly fall dead or flight away from the rest of the covey to land and possibly run a few yards before keeling over stone-dead. Alternatively, a pheasant may be seen to set its wings and flight into a tree to perch for a few moments before falling to the ground dead. Pigeons may have a somewhat similar reaction. Grouse on the other hand will usually plunge into the heather and will be found near where they were seen to land. It is always worth watching any game that has shown signs of being hit and following it up to the point where it was seen to land, then casting the dog on the line. It is surprising how much game may be retrieved in this way on the roughshoot which might otherwise have been lost to the bag. Even if nothing is found it is always worth trying. The roughshooter with a reliable dog should seldom leave wounded game unpicked, but there will always be an occasional mysterious failure even with the best of dogs.

Failure to Retrieve

There are many reasons for a dog's failure on a bird, or on ground game. It is always worth giving the dog the benefit of the doubt if it normally has a good nose and for no particularly obvious reason fails on what seems a simple retrieve. If it happens just once the answer may simply be that the particular bird, for one reason or another, was carrying very little or no scent. Sometimes birds shot in the backside do leave very little scent, perhaps because the scent gland has been blocked. Or it may simply be very bad scenting conditions where that particular bird has fallen. There may be a great deal of pollen, dust or mould in that patch of roots getting in the dog's nose and interfering with its scenting powers. There may be fallen leaves with a touch of frost still on them carrying no scent of the bird that has just run over them. Or again the bird may have entered water and left no scent behind in that shallow stream.

Given an intelligent cast down wind by his handler the dog may pick up the scent again in some of these instances and find the bird after all. It is in understanding the problems and helping his dog when required and not mindlessly berating him when he is doing his best that the superior handler shows his understanding and sympathy with his dog. It is essential, however, that the rough-shooter understands the game and its likely behaviour before he can hope to anticipate his dog's reactions in the field.

Bird Reactions

If a bird is wing tipped it may fly a long way before coming down to ground and it is important to know the bird's likely reactions on landing. Pheasants and partridges will almost certainly run on landing unless hit in the body as well. Woodcock will also tend to run on landing in these circumstances. A snipe will crouch on landing and usually try to take off again when the dog comes up. Grouse and pigeons may run a short distance but will usually be found fairly close to where they were marked on landing. If a bird is flying well and strongly but has a leg down it may well recover, although every effort should be made to find it. If it has both legs down and is flying erratically indicating a serious body wound it will not get up again and should be marked carefully and the dog then cast on the line. An experienced dog will often know instinctively when a bird has been hit and an experienced handler may be able to judge by its reactions.

Wildfowl Reactions

Both ducks and geese when wounded, if they land on water will almost immediately head for the cover on the shore. If they come down on land they will head for the nearest water. As with any birds when it is thought they may have been hit, it is important to keep an eye on them as they fly off. After a shot at a skein of geese they may sometimes be seen to start planing down as if to land some distance away and then suddenly scatter upwards in confusion. This almost invariably means that the lead bird was hard hit and when it started losing height the rest of the skein followed it down until it finally fell dead, when they scattered skywards. If this is seen it is well worth marking the spot and taking the dog towards it. The likelihood is that the leading bird will be found stone-dead at any-thing up to half a mile or more away.

Leaving it to the Dog

By marking the fall of a bird and getting the dog onto it smartly the roughshooter can help him considerably, but he must be careful not to interfere unduly. If the dog marks the fall and then strikes a line that is fine, and it is best to leave him. Once sent on the line and showing interest it is best to leave a good dog to get on with it rather than interfere and possibly call him off the right line. Depending on the bird shot and its probable reactions, the roughshooter may urge him to search around the marked fall or follow up any line indicated. It is generally as well in such circumstances, however, to rely on your dog.

Once the dog has learned by experience and knows what is required, it is better to leave matters to him and not interfere. If he seems to be going right out of the field that is probably because that winged cock pheasant or partridge has headed for the cover of the hedge and is running like a stag. To call the dog back then is an act of sheer stupidity and the chances are that if he obeys orders and comes off the line he will subsequently fail to recover the bird through no fault of his own. Nor is he going to be helped if his handler, or anyone else, walks across the fall of the bird and fouls the scent. Similarly, sending two or even three dogs to find a bird, or several birds near to each other at the same time is only certain to lead to confusion with rival handlers whistling their dogs and a state of general chaos reigning which frequently ends with no bird being retrieved at all.

Once a dog has started working and is showing signs of interest, as long as he knows his business the handler should bear in mind that he is now the non-working partner. This is the dog's part of the proceedings, where his instincts and senses are superior to those of his handler. Even if the handler is sure he saw the bird going one way and the dog appears to be working in the wrong direction it is better to leave it to him. More often than not it will be found that the bird has doubled back and he will be calling the dog off the right line and it will be lost.

In Field Trials

Something often seen in field trials is when under the stress of the moment even the experienced handler fails to trust his dog and calls it off a scent when it is showing every sign of being successful. Since the judge is judging the dog not the handler it is open to question whether he should interfere and tell the handler to leave his dog alone. Some field trial judges of course may be good dog handlers themselves and efficient enough judges of dog handling without necessarily knowing very much about game. This is bound to be a considerable handicap, however, since they will not always fully understand what is happening. I heard a well-known female judge, who quite often picks up, but does not shoot, during the course of a spring working test in March refer to a mallard performing the typical trailing wing act to lead a dog away from its nest as 'a wounded duck'. I suppose she knew the shooting season was over, but clearly she had never seen a bird during the nesting season. Without a full understanding of the ways of game the roughshooter, like that field trial judge, is likely to miss a great deal when his dog is working.

Shooting Runners

In one respect especially the roughshooter can help his dog much more readily than a driven shooter. If the roughshooter sees a runner in full view and a safe shot may be taken he should without hesitation shoot. There is no point in losing game or wasting time unnecessarily. This especially applies where wildfowl, geese or ducks may be seen swimming on the surface of the water. Ducks especially, after initially winging across the surface, will often dive and continue diving, giving the dog a hard and difficult chase. A dog that will follow a duck underwater is an advantage, but it can also be something of a worry where there are weeds or wire in which it may become entangled. A good water dog, however, which can follow scent on water and find those ducks tucked into the bank is a very useful asset, but if the roughshooter can save it the trouble with a timely shot he is merely fulfilling his role in the partnership. This is simply a matter of training and experience both of dog and roughshooter.

Gaining Experience

No dog can be expected to work automatically. Like humans they require training and experience, not only on the different game they are likely to encounter, but also on the different sorts of ground. They should not for instance be expected to swim immediately, although many dogs will take readily to water. Equally they cannot be expected to quarter far out on a moor when they have always walked to heel. Nor can they be expected to stay within range in roots unless they have practised this beforehand. It is a never-ceasing source of amazement to me how people can expect their dogs to behave well under circumstances which are totally strange to them with no preparation beforehand. It should be obvious that a dog which has always worked in the open will require time to get used to working in the close confines of a wood, or in the totally strange surroundings to him of a field of kale, when he has never experienced this before. In such circumstances a dog should never be berated for wild behaviour. It is not his fault, but his handler's for not giving him sufficient prior experience and training.

Reasons for Poor Work

When a dog is obviously not working well, is failing for instance to make retrieves that seem perfectly simple and is misbehaving generally there is no point in just cursing it. There is usually a perfectly sound reason if the handler cares to think it out. If a bitch it may be coming into season, in which case they may often behave in a very flighty and disobedient fashion. Alternatively, if a dog there may be a bitch in season in the area, or even out on the shoot, although handlers with bitches coming into season should always leave them at home rather than take them out and possibly spoil everyone else's sport as the dogs crowd round her and refuse to work.

There is also always the possibility that the dog may be sickening for something and, just like a human in similar circumstances, may be feeling ill and unable to work properly. The dog may have caught a chill and be feeling unfit to work. Or it may have been inhaling exhaust fumes in the back of the car and consequently be unable to scent anything. Sometimes a long journey to a shoot or strange overnight accommodation may have left the dog feeling out of sorts. There is usually an explanation when a good dog has a bad day.

It may even be something quite silly, but again not the dog's fault, such as having been fed a cheese sandwich by one of the guns during the lunch break, causing total loss of scenting abilities. No one should ever feed someone else's dog in this way, nor should dogs be allowed to sit around looking for food, but these things do happen. It is always advisable to put the dog back in the car, or out of the way, during such intervals in the shooting.

Lameness

If the dog is seen to be going lame the handler should not continue to work it. Have a look at it and try to find out the reason. It may simply be a thorn in the pad, which is easily removed. The dog may have pulled a muscle, or more seriously damaged a tendon, or it may have cut or spiked itself on barbed wire. If it is not obviously serious simply put it on the lead and keep it at heel. If it is serious get it back to the car as soon as possible and if necessary straight to the vet. Obviously a small cut on the pad is not very important but a bad rip on barbed wire which needs stitching is better seen to as soon as possible and a pulled tendon is also a serious matter requiring immediate attention. Only a certifiable idiot would continue to try to work his dog in such circumstances, but unfortunately there are quite a few around. Anyone who tries to prove their own toughness at the expense of their dog merely proves their own stupidity.

Safety First

It is always important to have especial care when shooting over dogs working in front of the guns, but there is much more than that to safety with gun or rifle. An accidental discharge from a loaded shotgun or rifle can kill or maim humans as well as animals. The safety catch should only be set in the Fire position as the shotgun or rifle is raised to the shoulder. It is desirable to get into this habit and to have the safety catch on Safe at all other times. But that in itself is not enough. **Never** carry a loaded shotgun or rifle unless it is about to be used. **Always** unload when crossing obstacles and whenever shooting is over. Make sure that no ricochet from wires, water or stones, or even trees, could possibly endanger life or limb of man or dog. Always be on the look out for dogs, stock and people in unexpected places. **Never** shoot where you cannot see clearly. **Be careful at all times.**

At the End of the Day

After the day's sport it is important if the dog is wet that it should be dried before being put in the car. An old towel should be kept for the purpose. This is not pampering the dog in any way, since it will work longer and will not suffer rheumatism or arthritis and have to be retired prematurely if such a precaution is taken. Nor should the roughshooter spend an hour or so in a pub discussing the day while his dog waits in the cold car. In particular he should not leave the dog lying cold, wet, tired and hungry beside a pile of freshly shot game. This is asking for trouble, although it is often seen. Despite its soft mouth or field trial qualifications, this is asking for the dog to eat the game and I have known owners, who should have known better, surprised to find their dog halfway through a hare or pheasant on their belated return to their car. The roughshooter should get the dog back home as soon as possible and, after looking him over to make sure he has no cuts or sores, as well as removing any burrs or ticks that may have been picked up, he should feed him. Once the dog has been fed and kennelled in clean fresh straw the gun should be cleaned and the roughshooter may then start looking after himself, but the dog comes first. A good dog deserves care and attention from his owner. He will work all the better for it and probably live longer.

The Source of Good Sport

In general the roughshooter will find that to a very great extent his sport is governed by the ability, or lack of it, of his dog. If the dog is not good at hunting and cannot find game in the first place then the roughshooter will find his sport accordingly poor. If it is a good hunter but will not retrieve, or is a poor retriever, then again the roughshooter will find himself losing out. There are indeed few things more infuriating than the dog which refuses to look for game which has been seen to fall. The roughshooter without a good working dog obviously cannot expect to enjoy nearly such good sport as the roughshooter who has put time and trouble into choosing or breeding a good dog and training it well. A good dog is the source of good sport on the roughshoot. While no-one will get much more out of any roughshoot than they are prepared to put into it, a sound all-round working dog is the foundation stone of the good sporting roughshoot.

Glossary

Acknowledge flush, of hunting dog: To drop to the flush of game.

Antlers, of deer: The horny outgrowth on the heads of males; rare in females.

Back, of pointer, or setter: To honour the point of another and come on point also.

Bag: The amount of 'game' and 'various' shot during the day.

B.A.S.C.: British Association for Shooting and Conservation. Formerly the Wildfowlers' Association of Great Britain and Ireland, it seeks to advance in every way the aims of all those interested in shooting.

Beaters: Those who drive the game over the guns on a driven day.

Beater's gun: One who walks with the line of beaters to shoot birds breaking back over the line.

Bender: A wire snare attached to a bent hazel wand so set that when an animal disturbs the snare it releases the wand which straightens and leaves the animal dangling.

B.F.S.S.: British Field Sports Society, a society aimed at the furtherance of all field sports.

Blackgame, or Black grouse: *Tetrao tetrix*: Divided by sex into blackcock and grey-hen.

Blown pattern: Where the shot is widely scattered leaving large gaps through which game might fly unscathed; common with faulty loading or sometimes with high velocity cartridges.

Block, of forestry plantation: An area generally delineated by broad rides or fire-breaks.

Blue hare: *Lepus timidus Scoticus*: Found in hill country; bluish colouring in summer turning white in winter.

Bore, or gauge: The inside of the barrel of a shotgun above the cartridge chamber. The size is gauged by the number of pure lead spherical balls of a size fitting the diameter of the bore which weigh one pound, i.e. 12 balls, 12-bore: Any bore smaller than 32 is given by the measurements of the diameter in decimals of the inch. The commonest is .410 (inches).

Brace, of game: Two; a couple.

Brace-work, of gundogs: Two working in unison.

Break cover, of ground game: In front of dogs or beaters, to leave the shelter of cover and enter open ground.

Brown: To fire into the centre of a covey or flock of birds without selecting an individual bird; i.e. fire into 'the brown'.

Buck: The male of Chinese water deer, fallow, muntjac, or roe; also of hare or rabbit.

Burr, of antlers. The rough outer edge of the coronet.

Butt: When driving grouse, a prepared position for the gun to stand when awaiting driven grouse. May also apply in relation to partridges or wildfowl.

Butterfly shots, of wildfowlers: Derisive term referring to fair-weather shooters.

Cage trap, for birds: Wire netting cage usually on lobsterpot principle, for birds.

Calf, of deer: Young of red, or sika.

Cartridge adaptor: A thin cylinder slipping inside cartridge chamber enabling cartridges of smaller bore, or gauge, to be used in the gun.

Cartridge extractor: Small tool with three claws to fit over cartridge cap enabling a swollen or damaged cartridge stuck in the chamber to be withdrawn easily.

Cast, of stag, or buck: To shed antlers.

Cheeper: A young game bird.

Choke, of a shotgun: Very slight constriction towards the end of the barrels which concentrates the shot.

Clap, of game: To lie frozen or squatting to avoid danger. A common trait.

Clean, of a stag's or buck's antlers: When free of velvet.

Clean delivery, of a gundog: When presenting game to its handler without fuss or mouthing.

Clean pick-up, of gundog: Steady retrieve without mouthing or hesitation.

Clean weight, of deer: When entire viscera has been removed but with head and feet still attached.

Close season, of all game: The period when it is illegal to shoot or hunt.

Coccidiosis: A parasitic, common disease of game birds, generally fatal; hares and rabbits have their own types.

Cock: A male bird, or (colloq.) a woodcock.

Cocks only day: A shooting day either at start or, more commonly, end of season when only cock pheasants are shot.

Coronet, of deer: The base of the antler adjoining the pedicle.

Covert: A wood, thicket, or gorse patch.

Covey, of grouse or partridges: A family group.

Decoy: A dead bird, or dummy, set out in a lifelike manner to attract others of the same species.

Deer forest: A stretch of hillside where deer may be found; need not have any trees.

Doe: Female of Chinese water deer, fallow, muntjac and roe; also of hare and rabbit.

Double-barrel, of shotgun: May be over-and-under, or side-by-side; former favoured by trap shooters; may be side-lock or box-lock, ejector, or non-ejector, sliding breech or hammer.

Draw-on, of gundog, esp. pointer or setter: To advance steadily towards game while on point.

Drive: A part of the day's sport at driven game when on a single piece of ground, covert or crop beaters are to drive game over the guns. The day is made up of a series of drives.

Driven game: Game driven by beaters so that it passes over the waiting guns.

Ejector gun: A gun with individual extractors to eject a cartridge when fired.

Fag, of red deer: A small stag accompanying an older beast.

Fairweather shot (colloq.): One who stays indoors when it is raining or finds an excuse not to shoot.

False point, of pointer or setter: A point made where there is found to be no game.

Feed hopper: A hopper used for holding grain or pellets, for feeding game; may be home-made from old oil cans, or similar containers; placed in ride or place where game may be taught to feed from it during the winter months.

Feed stack: A pile of tailings placed on a hurdle or similar base resting on two straw bales makes a simple feed stack, providing a feeding place for gamebirds and a base to scratch.

Fenn trap: Approved humane type of spring trap.

Ferret: Near relative to polecat; used for bolting rabbits; male known as hob, female as jill.

Flankers, of beaters: Experienced beaters with flags on poles whose job is to walk on either flank of beating party and turn any covey or grouse or partridges forward over the waiting guns by waving flag should they appear to be attempting to fly back or sideways.

Flash: A small pool, or pond, possibly the result of heavy rain or floodwater to which wildfowl are often attracted.

Flighting: The act of shooting wildfowl or pigeons as they flight in to feed or roost at dawn or dusk.

Flush: To cause game to take flight or break cover.

Flushing point: A place where game birds are forced to take flight from a covert when being driven forward, either by strategically-placed wire netting, or sewelling (see sewelling).

Foreshore cowboys (colloq.): Derisive wildfowling term for novices who fire at any bird in sight in or out of range.

Form: The name for the scrape or hollow in which a hare lies.

Forward allowance: The theoretical amount allowed in front of a crossing bird when swinging the gun and pulling the trigger; must vary with each individual.

Fouling: The deposit left in the gun after barrels have been fired.

Fray, of deer: To rub the antlers against a tree, post or stone, especially to get rid of velvet, or later during the rut.

Frenchman (colloq.): The red-legged partridge.

Game bag: Bag used for carrying game; traditional British type has broad strap for carrying over shoulder; waistcoat types may be preferred.

Gamebirds: Those birds listed as gamebirds are: Blackgame (i.e. blackcock and grey-hen), Capercaillie, or Capercailzie, Grouse, Pheasant, Partridges, Ptarmigan, Snipe, Woodcock.

Game book: Contains a record of each shooting day.

Game Conservancy: An association formed for the advancement of knowlege about British game, its care and management, for the general improvement of shooting. Based at Fordingbridge, Hampshire.

Game Licence: A licence to shoot game obtainable from the Post Office.

Game shooting season: The periods during which game may be shot are as follows:

> **Grouse:** August 12th to December 10th
>
> **Blackgame:** August 20th to December 10th
>
> **Partridge:** September 1st to February 1st
>
> **Pheasant:** October 1st to February 1st
>
> **Capercailzie:** October 1st to January 31st
>
> **Snipe:** August 12th to January 31st
>
> **Woodcock:** In Scotland, September 1st to January 31st. In England and Wales, October 1st to January 31st
>
> **Ground game,** i.e. Hares and Rabbits: May be shot throughout the year, but hares may not be sold between March and July inclusive and on moorland or unenclosed land may be shot only by the occupier or those authorised by him between December 11th (July 1st in Scotland) and March 31st.

Game-shot, or game-shooter: One who shoots gamebirds, either driven or walking up.

Gin trap: Form of leghold trap, now illegal, based on old-fashioned man trap, used principally for rabbits and small ground predators.

Going back, of deer: Deteriorating through age or illness; may also be applied to antlers.

Gralloch, of deer: Removing the stomach and intestines from newly shot deer.

Gun: In shooting, refers also to man carrying the gun, i.e. the shooter.

Half duck (colloq.): Teal.

Hand-reared: Of game birds reared by hand or under a broody hen or in an incubator rather than in the wild; common with pheasants, partridges and mallard.

Heel scent: The track leading away from game, often followed by an inexperienced young gundog.

Herd, of deer: A group.

Hide: An artificial place of concealment for the gun when waiting for wildfowl, pigeons, etc. May be made from straw bales or netting, etc., but should blend with surroundings and conceal gun from view.

High seat: A raised platform from which to observe or shoot deer, generally in or on the edge of woodland.

Hind: Female of red and sika deer.

Hob, of ferret: A male.

Hock, of ground game: To nick the hind tendon after legging to prevent the leg slipping through.

Hold Game, of gundogs: To hold game fixed when pointing staunchly.

Hummel, of red deer: A stag without antlers; possibly due to accident or injury; should always be culled when seen.

Inside span, of antlers: The widest measurement between main beams.

In velvet: Of male deer when antlers are still growing and are covered with a soft furry outer skin.

Jack: Male hare.

Jill, of ferret: Female.

Jug, jouk, or juk: Of partridge, or pheasants occasionally, to roost on the ground.

Jugging circle: The circle of droppings left by a covey of partridges after jugging, or jouking.

Kid: The young of roe deer.

Kindle, of rabbits: To bear young.

Kite-hawk: A kite shaped like a hawk sometimes used to keep game down when very wild, on moor or downland; inadvisable to use too often as may drive birds off ground.

Knobber, of red deer: Young male in second year; also knobbler.

Leash, of game: Three of a species.

Leg, of ground game: To slit one hind leg above the hock and slip the other leg through it for convenience of carriage. It is usual to leg in pairs so that the pairs may be thrown over a pole balancing each other and for ease in counting.

Lek, of blackgame: The elaborate mating dance of black cocks, hence lekking ground, lekking.

Lie-up of ferrets: When a ferret remains down a rabbit hole and refuses to return to the surface.

Line-ferret: A ferret attached to a knotted cord used to locate a lie-up; now generally superseded by direction finders attached to collar, or harness.

Long drop, of gundog: The drop at a distance from handler to whistle or command.

Magnum: A term loosely applied to any bore of shotgun of any kind which is chambered for a heavier than normal load.

Mark: To note where game falls when shot.

Melanistic mutant, of pheasant: Notable for dark plumage in both sexes and for pale soles to feet; now widespread.

Nye, of pheasants: A family group such as might come from a single nest.

Pack, of grouse or partridges: To form large groups, usually after being driven a number of times; usually segregated into cocks and hens; may amount to as many as 100 or more birds depending on numbers on ground.

Pair, of grouse and partridges: To Mate.

Parcel, of hinds: A group.

Partnership, of shooting: A shoot shared by two or more people on a partnership basis.

Patch: Linen square used to clean shotgun after use, fitting on jag of cleaning rod.

Pattern, of shotgun: The density of shot at the target, measured by plating the shotgun; i.e. measuring the number of pellets and evenness of pattern in a 30 inch circle at 40 yards when fired at whitewashed steel plate.

Paunch: To gut a rabbit; should be done soon after shooting; insert knife under apex of ribs and run down to haunch without piercing intestines, hook finger under the stomach then turn out stomach and intestines with twist of wrist. Hares should not be paunched.

Pearling, of antlers: The rough formation of beam and burr.

Pedicle, of antlers: The bone from which a stag or buck's antlers grow.

Peg, of a gundog: to seize squatting game instead of flushing it.

Pitting, of inside of shotgut barrels: Corrosion due to lack of careful cleaning after use.

Plane, of gamebirds, generally pheasants: To glide downwards with set wings.

Plate of shotgun: To fire at whitewashed steel plate at 40 yards to check pattern within 30 inch circle.

Poach, of game: To kill game on another's preserves without permission, with gun, bow, net, trap or dog; to take game illegally.

Poacher: One who takes game illegally on another's ground; alt: derisive term used to describe a greedy shot.

Poacher's pocket: Capacious game pocket inside lining of shooter's jacket.

Point, of gundogs: To indicate the presence of game by a rigid stance; hence, to be on point.

Poke, of shooting: To aim the shotgun instead of swinging with flying or running game, a serious fault almost certainly resulting in a miss.

Poult: A half-grown pheasant.

Prick, of game: To wound with pellets from a shotgun instead of killing cleanly; game may recover or die later; should be retrieved if possible; hence, pricked bird.

Proof-marks: The records of proving by the Proof House stamped on the barrels after testing the shotgun. It is illegal to sell a shotgun without modern proof marks and it may be highly dangerous to use a gun with outdated proof marks with modern powders.

Pronking, of fallow deer: The typical stiff-legged bouncing gait of fallow when alarmed.

Pull-through: A weighted cord used to pull cleaning materials through a shotgun or rifle instead of a cleaning rod.

Purse-net: A net designed to fit over rabbit holes, formed like an old fashioned draw-string purse. When pegged in position the rabbit bolts from the hole and the strings draw the net tight around it.

Quarter, of gundogs: To cover ground efficiently in front of the guns to find game.

Quarry, of hunt, or stalker: Animal hunted or stalked; derived from the word Quyrreye, or entrails, originally fed to the hounds after the hunt.

Ribs, of shotgun: The steel strips between the two barrels of a side-by-side double-barrelled shotgun. Known as top rib and bottom rib.

Right and left (colloq.): Two birds killed by successive shots fired without the gun leaving the shoulder, i.e. the gun is swung cleanly from one target to the next without appreciable pause.

Road out, of gundogs: To work out a scent to ensure that game has all gone after being flushed.

Roar, of a stag: To bellow; the sound made during the rut by the red stag.

Rocketer (colloq.), usually of pheasants: A fast-climbing and accelerating game bird, coming over the guns high and at speed.

Roller, of deer: When shot on steep hillside and falls and rolls so far, venison is useless.

Rough shoot: A shoot where no full-time keeper is maintained and where game is not reared on any great scale, nor regularly driven by organised teams of beaters.

Royal, of red stag: A head with twelve points.

Rubbish, of deer: Poor deer which should be culled.

Run, generally of groundgame: Regular worn track left by rabbit or hare, also sometimes predators or other game.

Run-in, of gundog: To run forwards without orders after game which has been flushed or shot.

Runner, of gamebirds: A bird which has been shot, generally in the wing, but is still capable of running, often for considerable distances and at considerable speed.

Rut, of deer: The mating season.

Safety catch: A slide, generally on the top of the stock, which merely acts as a check on the triggers. The shotgun or rifle should always be unloaded when not in use and the safety catch should always be on Safe except when raised to the shoulder ready for use.

Saltings: Salt water marsh, or meadows flooded by seawater; very attractive to wildfowl.

Scrub rabbit (colloq.): A rabbit which habitually lies out in the open in a scrape, or form, like a hare, rather than in a burrow.

Seat: The scrape where a rabbit lies in the open.

Self-hunting, of gundogs: The bad vice of going off to hunt hedgerows and fields for game by itself; difficult to eradicate once started.

Swelling, or sewin: A cord knotted at intervals with cloth, or plastic, used to flush pheasants at a flushing point, or act as stop.

Shed, of buck or stag: To cast antlers.

Shoot: An area of country over which shooting rights are held by a person, a partnership or a syndicate.

Shoot management: The efficient control and organisation of a shoot, including game rearing and preservation.

Shot: The pellets used in a shotgun cartridge, generally of chilled lead shot and of varying sizes.

Shot size: The size of the shot or pellets, used in the cartridge of a shotgun; should vary with the size of the quarry.

Shot stringing: The formation of the shot column after leaving the barrels is known as shot stringing; at 40 yards may be as much as 8 feet.

Slot: The footprint of a deer.

Snare: A noose trap, generally of wire, in the form of a running noose; may be for rabbits or foxes.

Stag: A male red or sika deer from 4th year on.

Stop: A beater stationed at the edge of a covert to prevent birds breaking out; by tapping gently with a stick he should keep them within the covert.

Strong on the wing: Of young game birds able to fly strong and boldly early in the season.

Swing: To move the gun across the body at the speed of a crossing bird, or faster.

Switch: Malshapen antlers of a stag, with only 2 or at most 4 points, providing murderous killing effect; should be culled whenever seen.

Syndicate shoot: Shoot shared by a group of sportsmen forming a group to share expenses. Each syndicate will have their own rules and regulations regarding their shooting and the number of days shot, etc.

Tailor (colloq.): To wound game rather than kill cleanly.

Tealer: The wooden cleft stick to support the wire of a snare.

Tight pattern: Of a shotgun pattern which shows a concentration of shot well within the 30 inch circle.

Tine: Each point or branch of a stag's antlers, also termed point.

Towered bird: A gamebird which flies almost perpendicularly upwards after being shot in the lung or spine and then falls stone dead.

Tunnel trap: A trap set in a covered run, set to catch small predators such as stoats and weasels.

Turk's head: Woollen mop attachment to shotgun cleaning rod for oiling barrels.

Various: Any species of birds or animals not specifically mentioned in the columns of a game register may be so called.

Velvet: The skin covering the antlers during growth; hence, in velvet.

Venison: The meat of deer.

Walk up, of game shooting: To walk in line with guns and beaters to shoot partridges, grouse, etc.

Warfarin: The trade name for an effective poison used against rats and squirrels.

Waster: Of a deer that is sickly or ill.

Wildfowl: From a wildfowler's viewpoint, those ducks and geese which may be shot inland from September 1st to January 31st or on the foreshore from September 1st to February 20th. **Ducks:** Common Pochard, Gadwall, Goldeneye, Mallard, Pintail, Shoveller, Teal, Tufted Duck, Wigeon: **Geese:** Canada, Greylag, Pinkfoot, Whitefront (in England and Wales only: fully protected in Scotland).

Wildfowling: The act of flight shooting wildfowl. Exact definitions vary: some wildfowlers use the term only to mean shooting on tidal land, others include inland marshes too.

Winged bird: A bird shot in the wing and incapable of flying.

Winter feed: for game birds, and deer, set out during the winter months, in straw rides, hoppers or feed stacks, to supplement the natural feeding in hard conditions and attract game to the ground.

Wisp; or snipe: A group.

Yeld, of red deer: A hind that has not bred the previous year but is not necessarily barren.

Zern: A sufficient measure of malt whisky taken after a day's shooting, stalking, hunting or fishing to induce contemplative discussion of the day; hence, a Zernful.

Critical Bibliography

Arnold, Richard. *Pigeon Shooting*. Faber, 1956
Always a good writer on sport and this is one of his earlier works, updated in 1976 by Kaye & Ward.

Baker, Max. *Sport with Woodpigeons. Shooting Times*, 1934
The first book devoted entirely to pigeon shooting as a sport. Now dated, but worth reading.

Bateman, James A. *Animal Traps and Trapping*. David & Charles, 1971
Comprehensive study of traps and trapping from the earliest days of mankind to the present with numerous illustrations.

Brander, Michael. *The Roughshooter's Dog*. 1st published 1957, republished Gentry Books, 1971, reprinted 1974, 1978
Useful guide to training the pointer-retriever gundog; first in English language.

The Roughshooter's Sport. Macgibbon & Kee, 1957
Now very dated guide to roughshooting. Well illustrated and still has some points of value

Groundgame. 1st published 1963, republished Tideline, 1978
Useful guide to ground game, rabbits and hares found in U.K. Originally part of S.T. Library

Gundogs, their Care and Training. 1st published A & C Black, 1963, reprinted 1969, 1972, 1976, second edition 1983
Small but concise guide to the care and training of a gundog from choosing a pup through to field trials.

The Concise Guide to Game Shooting. 1st published 1965, republished The Sportsmans Press, 1986, revised edition 1988.

A Dictionary of Sporting Terms. A & C Black 1968
Covers all forms of hunting, shooting, fishing, falconry, deer stalking and associated field sports.

Training the Pointer-Retriever Gundog. Pelham Books, 1983
A guide to the pointer-retriever gundogs from choosing the breed and pup to training to field trial standard.

Deer Stalking in Britain. The Sportsman's Press, 1986

A useful all-round guide to deer stalking in the U.K. well illustrated by Christopher Wood

Sporting Pigeon Shooting. A & C Black, 1986
Useful guide to pigeon shooting in U.K. on various levels from treetops and ground, also quarry and clifftop shooting.

Brander, Michael, and Ed Zern (joint editors). *An International Encyclopedia of Shooting.* Rainbird/Pelham, 1972, Peerage Books, 1982
An international directory of shooting, very well illustrated. Covers game large and small.

Cadman, Arthur. *Dawn, Dusk and Deer.* Country Life, 1966
Gifted writer and authority on deer conveying his enthusiasm. Well illustrated by C. F. Tunnicliffe

Carlisle, G. L. and Percy Stanbury. *Shotguns and Shooter.* Barrie & Jenkins, 1970, reprinted 1973, 1977, 1978, revised edition 1981
This has some good points of note for the roughshooter as well as for the general game shooter, even if a little dated.

Chalmers, Patrick R. *Field Sports of Scotland.* Philip Allan, 1936
Some very practical points and, as always, delightfully written.

Coats, Archie. *Amateur Keeper.* Studio Vista, 1962
Good introduction to keepering for the amateur on a small scale, with some very sound advice for all shooters.

Coats, Archie. *Pigeon Shooting.* Studio Vista, 1963, republished Andre Deutsch, 1972
This is a book on the subject by a professional who has spent much of his life at the task.

Coles, C. L. *Shooting and Stalking.* Stanley Paul
A comprehensive guide with others to various aspects of shooting and stalking

Coles, Charles, L. *Shooting Pigeons.* S. T. Library, 1963
One of these small Shooting Times Library editions; all excellent for their purpose.

Dawson, Kenneth. *Just an Ordinary Shoot.* 1st published 1935, republished Country Life, 1938, new edition 1949
Evergreen classic with splendid illustrations by Winifred Austen. Now somewhat dated for the roughshooter.

Drought, Captain J. B. *Successful Shooting.* Country Life, 1948
Although a post-war publication this has an old-fashioned air, but some good material nonetheless.

Humphreys, John. *Hides, Calls and Decoys.* Percival Marshall, 1978
A fairly comprehensive review of the majority of decoys and calls available with a sound section on hides.

Humphreys, John. *Modern Pigeon Shooting.* Tideline, 1980
Sound advice with pictures of almost all types of decoy taken by D. Parfitt.

Jackson, Tony. *Shotguns and Shooting*. Ward Lock, 1982
A simple and well illustrated introduction to shooting by an ex-editor of *Shooting Times*.

Johnson, A. E. B. *Shooting Wood-Pigeons*. Jenkins, 1961, Boydell, 1980
Now somewhat dated but sound enough handbook of wood-pigeon shooting, mainly over decoys.

Lynn-Allen, Captain E. H. *Rough Shoot*. Hutchinson, 1942
Sub-titled: *Some thoughts for the Owner-Keeper*. Well illustrated by Master of Elphinstone. Dated, but good reading.

McCall, Ian. *Your Shoot Gamekeepering and Management*. A & C Black 1987
An excellent and extremely well illustrated introduction to the entire spectrum of game management.

Prior, Richard. *Living with Deer*. Andre Deutsch, 1965
Attractively written. Covers red, roe, fallow, sika and muntjac. Very readable with some good illustrations.

Sedgwick, Noel M. *Wildfowling and Roughshooting*. Herbert Jenkins, 1950.
By the foremost Editor of the *Shooting Times* and exponent of art. Always worth reading if now rather dated.

Smith, Guy N. *Gamekeeping and Shooting*. Spur Publications, 1982
Some interesting and on occasions quite controversial points of view, based primarily on a Forestry Commission Shoot.

Smith, Guy N. *Roughshooter's Handbook*. Boydell Press, 1988
Interesting account of shooting on Forestry Commission shoot. Dubious mention of shooting guinea fowl.

Swan, Mike. *Fowling for Duck*. Crowood Press, 1988
A readable and well illustrated practical guide to the pursuit of wild duck both on the shore and inland marshes.

Stanbury, Percy and Carlisle, G. L. *Shotgun and Shooter*. Barrie & Jenkins, 1970
Good all-round introduction to shooting and marksmanship and use of the shotgun in the field.

Tegner, Henry. *Game for the Sporting Rifle*. Herbert Jenkins, 1963
Always readable on hunting and stalking, this was perhaps one of his best books on the subject.

Tennyson, Julian. *Roughshooting*. A & C Black, 1938
Pleasantly pre-war approach to Roughshooting updated in the '50s and remains nostalgic.

Thurlow-Craig, C. W. *Shooter's Delight*. Hutchinson, 1952
A delightfully discursive account of roughshooting, wandering from S. America to Wales from 1914 to 1950.

Vesey-Fitzgerald, Brian. *British Game*. Collins, 1946
Profusely illustrated by editor of *The Field* and well known and experienced naturalist.

Whitehead, G. Kenneth. *Practical Deer Stalking*. Constable, 1986
Well known author of around a dozen books on deer of which this is
one of his best.